Lecture Notes of the Institute for Computer Sciences, Social Informatics and Telecommunications Engineering

458

More information about this series at https://link.springer.com/bookseries/8197

Teresa Pereira · John Impagliazzo ·
Henrique Santos (Eds.)

Internet of Everything

The First EAI International Conference,
IoECon 2022
Guimarães, Portugal, September 16–17, 2022
Proceedings

Springer

Editors
Teresa Pereira (iD)
University of Minho
Guimarães, Portugal

John Impagliazzo (iD)
Hofstra University
Hempstead, NY, USA

Henrique Santos (iD)
University of Minho
Guimarães, Portugal

ISSN 1867-8211   ISSN 1867-822X (electronic)
Lecture Notes of the Institute for Computer Sciences, Social Informatics
and Telecommunications Engineering
ISBN 978-3-031-25221-1   ISBN 978-3-031-25222-8 (eBook)
https://doi.org/10.1007/978-3-031-25222-8

This Springer imprint is published by the registered company Springer Nature Switzerland AG
The registered company address is: Gewerbestrasse 11, 6330 Cham, Switzerland

Preface

It is a pleasure to introduce the proceedings of the first edition of the 2022 European Alliance for Innovation (EAI) Internet of Everything Conference (IoECon). The Internet of Everything (IoE) is an emerging study area aimed at extending the IoT paradigms to their whole dimension, intelligently connecting devices, people, processes, data, and things. IoE is multi-disciplinary and offers an opportunity to explore the co-relations between different areas, techniques, and theories about a new cyber world. This first conference and the community it is assembling focus on a complete ecosystem that digitally interconnects everything, including people-to-people, people-to-machines, and machines-to-machines. IoECon has emphasized the technological effects on people, organizational processes, and the information security challenges from the accelerated technological evolution.

The technical program of IoECon 2022 consisted of ten out of thirteen accepted papers covering a wide set of technical and scientific areas, presented over two days within the main conference track. Aside from the high-quality technical paper presentations, the technical program also featured a keynote address, an invited talk, and a roundtable discussion. Ulrike Hugl, head of the scientific staff at the University of Innsbruck, Faculty of Business and Management, Austria, presented the keynote. It was a challenging view of the cyborg evolution and its potential impact. Honore Nyuyse, a general engineer at the Science and Technology Directorate agency within the Department of Homeland Security (DHS), USA, presented the invited talk, which showed a fascinating view of the strategy adopted by a large federal agency responsible for enforcing cybersecurity within a challenging transformation process. Henrique Santos moderated the roundtable discussion with the invited participation of Raúl Bordalo Junqueiro, head of Smart Cities and Business Development/Innovation point DST Group, Portugal, António Amaral from Polytechnic Institute of Porto, Portugal, and Natalie Kiesler from Leibniz-Institute für Bildungsforschung, Germany.

The EAI and the Information Systems Department of the Engineering School at the University of Minho supported the conference organization. Local arrangements and coordination with the general co-chairs, Henrique Santos and John Impagliazzo, were essential for the conference's success. I sincerely appreciated their constant support and guidance. It was also a great pleasure to work with such an excellent organizing committee team for their hard work in organizing and supporting the conference. We are also grateful to the conference managers, Kristina Havlickova and Elena Davydova from EAI, for their enthusiastic support and the authors who submitted their papers to the IoECon 2022 conference.

We strongly believe that the EAI IoECon conference provided an optimal forum for researchers, policymakers, developers, and practitioners to discuss all relevant science and technology aspects of IoE. We also expect to meet again at the IoECon 2023 conference, helping to make it an even more inspiring event for the consolidation of the IoE ecosystem and the development of an IoE community.

October 2022

Teresa Pereira
Henrique Santos
John Impagliazzo

Organization

Organizing Committee

General chair

Teresa Pereira — Information Systems Department, University of Minho, Portugal

General Co-chairs

John Impagliazzo — Hofstra University, New York, USA
Henrique Santos — Information Systems Department, University of Minho, Portugal

TPC Chair and Co-chair

Henrique Santos — Information Systems Department, University of Minho, Portugal

Steering Committee

Imrich Chlamtac — University of Trento, Italy

Publications Chairs

António Amaral — Polytechnic Institute of Porto, Portugal
Luís Barreto — Polytechnic Institute of Viana do Castelo, Portugal

Web Chair

Isabel Mendes — University of Aveiro, Portugal

Technical Program Committee

Hala Alrumaih — Imam Mohammad Ibn Saud Islamic University, Saudi Arabia
Casey Bennett — Hanyang University, School of Intelligence Computing, South Korea
Olga Bogoyavlenskaya — Petrozavodsk State University, Russia

Héctor Cancela	Universidad de la República, Uruguay
Juan (Jenny) Chen	National University of Defense Technology, China
Paolo Ciancarini	University of Bologna, Italy
Alison Clear	Eastern Institute of Technology, New Zealand
Ernesto Cuadros-Vargas	Latin American Center for Computing Studies (CLEI), Peru
Mats Daniels	Uppsala University, Sweden
Judith Gal-Ezer	Open University, Israel
Andrii Galkin	O.M. Beketov National University of Urban Economy, Kharkiv, Ukraine
Raúl Junqueira	DST Group, Portugal
Linda Marshall	University of Pretoria, South Africa
João Matos	DST Group, Portugal
Andrew McGettrick	Strathclyde University, UK
Simon	University of Newcastle, Australia
Shingo Takada	Keio University, Japan
Eliana Stavrou	University of Central Lancashire (UCLan), Cyprus
Gerrit van der Veer	Vrije Universiteit, Netherlands
Abhijat Vichare	ACM India, India

Contents

People-to-People

Perspectives on the Internet of Everything 3
  Natalie Kiesler and John Impagliazzo

Guidelines to Develop Consumers Cyber Resilience Capabilities in the IoE
Ecosystem 18
  Eliana Stavrou

A Competency Definition Based on the Knowledge, Skills, and Human
Dispositions Constructs 29
  Teresa Pereira, António Amaral, and Isabel Mendes

The Influence of the Image and Photography of E- Commerce Products
on the Purchase Decision of Online Consumers 39
  Manuel Sousa Pereira, António Cardoso, Carlota Fernandes,
  Sandra Rodrigues, and Frederico D'Orey

People-to-Machine and Machine-to-People

The Man-Machine Relationship on the Web: Motivation to Use the Internet 55
  Jorge Figueiredo, António Cardoso, Margarida Pocinho,
  and Isabel Oliveira

Cybersecurity Challenges in Healthcare Medical Devices 66
  Ana Longras, Teresa Pereira, and António Amaral

A WSN Real-Time Monitoring System Approach for Measuring Indoor
Air Quality Using the Internet of Things 76
  Elias Biondo, Thadeu Brito, Alberto Nakano, and José Lima

Scalability of IoT Systems: Do Execution Costs Predict the Quality
of Service? 91
  Ahmed Al-Qasmi, Huda Al Shuaily, Kennedy E. Ehimwenma,
  and Safiya Al Sharji

Machine-to-Machine

Transient Session Key Derivation Protocol for Key Escrow Prevention
in Public Key Infrastructure 103
   Vincent Omollo Nyangaresi, Zaid Ameen Abduljabbar,
   Ismail Yaqub Maolood, Mustafa A. Al Sibahee, Junchao Ma,
   and Abdulla J. Y. Aldarwish

Evaluating CoAP, OSCORE, DTLS and HTTPS for Secure Device
Communication 117
   Kristofer Nedergaard, Bhupjit Singh, and Birger Andersen

Author Index 133

People-to-People

Perspectives on the Internet of Everything

Natalie Kiesler[1]([✉]) [iD] and John Impagliazzo[2] [iD]

[1] DIPF Leibniz Institute for Research and Information in Education,
Frankfurt am Main, Germany
kiesler@dipf.de
[2] Hofstra University, Hempstead, NY, USA
john.impagliazzo@hofstra.edu

Abstract. In today's connected world, smartphones, watches, thermostats, and LEDs are a common feature of newly constructed buildings owned by not only technology enthusiasts but a majority of people. While the Internet of Things focuses on the connection of gadgets, the Internet of Everything (IoE) as a more holistic technology builds upon the idea of connecting devices, people, processes, data, and virtually everything via the internet. This paper provides an overview of the historical developments surrounding this evolving technology. Accordingly, the internet becomes a starting point and illustrates the steps towards a connected world. The ARPANET, mobile or connected devices, and the Internet of Things have fostered the consecutive stage – the IoE. It also outlines the current state of the art concerning its meaning, its effect on business models and research, and viewpoints toward future visions for education and other fields. The IoE is characteristic of the ambivalence of enormously high expectations and unresolved considerations that require intensive research and careful development in years to come.

Keywords: Internet of Everything · IoE ·
Things-people-data-processes · Historical overview · Future
perspectives · People-to-machines

1 Introduction

A brief shopping tour for smart home devices quickly illustrates the breadth of the currently available technologies and applications. The world faces a transformation in homes from heating, light, power, and home security control to weather or indoor climate sensors and household robots. In addition, it has never been easier to manage one's household and even chores via the internet or a mobile device. The idea to connect single-purpose physical devices to the internet and each other aims at the intersection of gathering data and utilizing them.

The Internet of Everything (IoE) as a recently emerging concept goes even beyond this understanding, as it connects not only devices but people, processes,

© ICST Institute for Computer Sciences, Social Informatics and Telecommunications Engineering 2023
Published by Springer Nature Switzerland AG 2023. All Rights Reserved
T. Pereira et al. (Eds.): IoECon 2022, LNICST 458, pp. 3–17, 2023.
https://doi.org/10.1007/978-3-031-25222-8_1

data, and things in an intelligent manner [17,37]. In this context, almost everything is online and connected via the internet, while data transfers (almost) occur in real-time. Moreover, due to content-based communication, artificial intelligence (AI), and machine learning, every interaction helps IoE devices become "smarter".

Therefore, the IoE has a greater scope and a broad range of possible future application scenarios, such as entertainment devices, distributed smart hardware, smart transportation systems or cities [35], and many more that cannot even list at this time point. The concept of IoE includes the Internet of Things (IoT) technology. It overlaps with ubiquitous computing, pervasive computing, industry 4.0, cognitive systems, the internet, communication protocols, cyber-physical systems, embedded systems, web 2.0, big data, and other related subject areas in computing.

This paper aims to provide a brief overview of the historical developments leading to the emergence of the IoE concept. This development comprises the emergence of the internet in the late 1960s, connected devices, the transition from fixed to mobile devices, and the Internet of Things. Furthermore, this work provides an overview of the IoE technology regarding its meaning, its effect on business models, and recent research on the IoE. It also outlines the importance of competency in IoE education and a vision of the IoE in the future.

2   Past Developments

The internet has been a persistent companion during the last decades for most people, even though its accessibility, appearance, and applications are constantly evolving. This section introduces some historical developments leading to the Internet of Everything that begins with the development of the technical

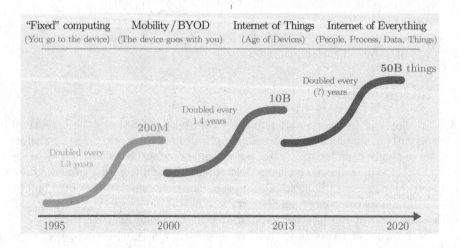

Fig. 1. Internet growth towards the IoE is occurring in waves [17].

foundation of the internet: The Advanced Research Projects Agency Network (ARPANET). The first connected devices, as well as the broad availability of mobile devices and WiFi, constitute further critical developmental stages culminating in the IoT as a precursor of the IoE (see Fig. 1) [17].

2.1 The Early Onset of Connected Devices

The internet has evolved through several stages since the late 1960s. These include academia (ARPANET), the informational stage (brochure ware), the transactional stage (e-commerce), and the social stage (web 2.0) [17]. Especially the ARPANET as a project on behalf of the U.S. Air Force constitutes a crucial starting point. It started in 1968 with a small group of researchers led by the Massachusetts Institute of Technology. It was the first network with distributed control. In 1977, the protocols TCP, and IP were first tested on ARPANET [18].

In the context of IoT and IoE, the connection of devices is of specific interest. For example, a Coke vending machine at Carnegie Mellon University was the first connected device. Students operated it, among them, David Nichols, a graduate student of computer science [1, 25]. Due to the high demand for soda and the long travel ways on campus, he wanted to track the machine's contents remotely. So he worked together with Ivor Durham and John Zsarnay and established a connection to the ARPANET in 1982. Anyone connected to the university's Ethernet could find out if soda cans were available and which ones were cold enough. At the time, Kazar used to joke about toasters being connected to the Internet [51].

In 1990, John Romkey did connect a toaster to the internet by using a TCP/IP protocol, which unleashed creativity among scientists. Web cameras started monitoring coffee machines in computer labs [25], and in 1997 the idea of an internet-connected refrigerator emerged. LG Electronics introduced the cooling device with a LAN port for IP connectivity in 2000. It allowed users online shopping and video calls [1, 25].

2.2 Mobile Devices and Expansion

With the emergence of mobile devices and wireless technology in the 2000s s and 2010s, connected devices started to upscale. In 2008, several big companies formed the Internet Protocol for Smart Objects Alliance and began to invest in respective research. Moreover, WiFi has become accessible to a significant number of people. The same is true for smart mobile devices [1]. Furthermore, in January 2010, Apple launched the first generation of the iPad [2].

Media coverage of connected devices and general interest increased at about the same time. The first international IoT conference occurred in Switzerland in 2008 and focused on Radio Frequency Identification (RFID) wireless communications over short distances and sensor networks. In the 2010s, the network layer protocol IPv6 emerged, and interconnected devices, such as thermostats, smart glasses, and light-emitting diodes (LEDs), were brought to the marketplace [25].

2.3 The Internet of Things

The label "Internet of Things" (IoT) was coined by Kevin Ashton in 1999 while working for Procter & Gamble. He used the term in the context of RFID-enabled device connectivity in the supply chain. The expression was supposed to attract the audience's attention [6,48]. In 2011, the IoT was added to the Gartner Hype Cycle for emerging technologies as "on the Rise" [19]. By now, the IoT refers to Internet-connected devices that can sense and share data, which is known as machine-to-machine (M2M) communication. Today, Internet Protocol (IP) forms a basis for IoT. The dictionary defines IoT as follows.

- "the networking capability that allows information to be sent to and received from objects and devices (such as fixtures and kitchen appliances) using the internet" [29]
- "objects with computing devices in them that are able to connect to each other and exchange data using the internet: Cloud applications will be used by billions of devices of all kinds, all connected to the internet of things. The internet of things might, for example, involve smart bins that can signal when they need to be emptied" [11]

The rapid evolution of the IoT has paved the way for further technological advances in numerous industries and markets, such as smart homes, transportation, cities, and healthcare. It connects things utilizing sensors, actuators, and network connectivity which allows them to collect and exchange data via the internet [43].

3 The Next Stage: IoE

The term "Internet of Everything", or IoE, was first used by CISCO's Dave Evans in 2012 [17] to describe a holistic concept of relevant and valuable connections between (1) people, (2) data, (3) processes, and (4) things. These "four pillars" are a novum compared to the IoT described by Weissberger [54], as IoT focuses mainly on the connections between things. However, it is still a relatively young term that is not widely known yet. Therefore, the IoE can also be perceived as the next stage of the IoT [15,48].

3.1 The Meaning of IoE

As depicted in Fig. 2, the IoE connects spaces such as people's homes with business and mobile settings. Connections to the internet include people-to-people (P2P), machine-to-machine (M2M), and people-to-machine (P2M) systems, while all of them comprise people, data, processes, and things. Thus, the IoE expands the communication channels beyond M2M communication in the IoT. According to Evans, the network effects create IoE's value and the opportunity for the internet's exponential growth and power. Eventually, individuals, businesses, and countries will be affected by the IoE as the gathered raw data

Internet of Everything

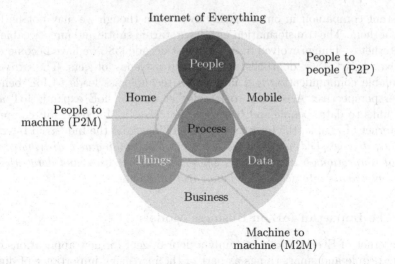

Fig. 2. The components of the Internet of Everything (IoE) [17].

becomes information. This activity is supposed to lead to learning processes, smarter decisions, and more effective control of the environment [17]. A CISCO study conducted in 2013 predicted a 14.4 trillion US$ value for net profit worldwide for the following decade [10]. It comprises the following key areas: asset utilization, employee productivity, supply chain and logistics, customer experience as well as innovation (including reducing time to market). In other words, the prediction is that IoE is a newly emerging and overly attractive market for businesses.

Nonetheless, CISCO's Chief Futurist describes the IoE as a technology that can benefit humanity, e.g., by making public communications more accessible via smart screens incorporating various modes of communication in real-time and offering WiFi to nearby devices. Conquering climate change utilizing sensors is one of the perspectives given in Evans' point of view for tomorrow. However, cooperation between government, organizations, businesses, and citizens is vital for overcoming the challenges of world hunger, water crises, and beyond [17]. Likewise, Mitchell et al. [35] suggest public policy goals, such as the monitoring of highways, education, and healthcare. Predicted barriers comprise technical challenges concerning network protocols (IPv6), power storage and energy capacities [17].

In 2015, Miraz et al. [31] note that the financial sector has already moved to mobile trading platforms by using smartphones and apps that IoE supports. Moreover, the expansion of cloud computing facilitates the connection of things, people, data, and processes in, for instance, shopping applications or mobile learning [24,32]. They assume that smart connections will determine the future. Due to the increasing urbanization by the 2050s, IoE will become a critical part of cities' infrastructures, and daily life [31]. Today, one can consider smart devices a constant companion in our everyday lives, even though we may not be fully aware of them. The transformation may have started subtle and unnoticeable. As the Internet of Things evolved during the last decade [38], we have become used to Alexa, smart TVs, doorbells, and other day-to-day objects. The explosion of available communication and interaction technologies leads to IoE being a broader perspective. According to Langley et al. [26], IoE expands IoT as it adds "links to data, people and (business) processes". Moreover, IoE comprises the Internet of People, the Internet of Nano Things, and the Industrial Internet.

Thus, it is possible to define the Internet of Everything as a distributed network of connections between people, smart things, processes, and data, whereas these components interact and exchange real-time data.

3.2   The Impact of IoE on Business Models

The Internet of Everything is certainly a door-opener for new applications connecting people and smart things as part of the increasing importance of digital technologies for value creation [9,21,23,28]. As IoE promises to change how we live, work, and interact, a significant number of industries and businesses require some remodeling to adapt and benefit from new opportunities related to smart things [50]. If smart things complement people's abilities, they can work on what they can do best and strive [27].

Langley et al. [26] review networked business models, service ecosystems, and how they organize their businesses. The resulting aspects concern the requirements for business transformation processes towards more value using IoE. For businesses, it is essential to consider the interoperability between systems and other industry partners, legacy processes and transactions, contracts, liability issues, security, data privacy, and the loss of control, to name a few [26]. In fact, the micro-, meso-, and macro-level of a service ecosystem are affected by a transformation towards IoE [39,41]. Another consequence is that current business models in individual industries may be fragmented and restructured due to overlapping systems and industries [40,52,55].

Fredette et al. [20] have outlined the perils and promises of hyper-connectivity as in IoE. Besides the suggested effects on social and professional organizations, neo-urbanization, (mobile) government (services), education, sustainability, and healthcare focus on businesses and the workforce. Furthermore, according to the Alcatel-Lucent report [20] as part of the World Economic Forum, the evolving IoE is going to affect the efficiency of supply chains positively. Supply and demand can be monitored and managed by employing sensors and machine-to-machine-to-human communications. The same is true for tracking inventories and the shipping of products. As a result, there is a significant reduction in human intervention, reducing costs and increasing profits.

Another aspect relates to the digitalization of human interaction within online social networks. For example, marketing and customer care need to take place on a new level (24/7) and via various online platforms and channels. In addition, expectations toward 99.9999 % of available services and systems and more are increasing. Therefore, platforms cannot fail in a hyper-connected business world. Similarly, workforces must face a significant shift towards mobile technologies and workplace settings. With increased broadband speeds, mobile devices, Web 2.0 tools, and applications, it has never been easier to work independently of a work location while collaborating with team members and customers. Also, the millennial generation is already using an interconnected environment, and they will embrace it as part of their work, which fosters the IoE transformation even further [20].

The IoE certainly has the potential to help transform today's business models and processes and to cause new cross-industry sectors and value chains in a globalized world. Depending on how smart things eventually become, networked business models will evolve. For example, Langley et al. [26] proposed a taxonomy of smart things based on their capabilities and their connectivity.

4   Recent Research on the IoE

Implementing the IoE comes with several challenges that, among others, affect the connection of billions of devices in terms of a smart network so that data can be gathered, analyzed, and shared, even distributed through users and devices. According to Shojafar and Sookhak [49], fog computing and cloud computing can provide the "network-plus-computing support by allowing the on-the-fly instantiation of software clones (e.g., virtual surrogates) of the physical sensing things onto resource-equipped nearby clouds (e.g., cloudlets) placed at the edge of the wireless access network" [49, p. 213]. Thus, dynamic local clouds might pose a solution with shorter service execution time and a greener computation and communication. At the same time, scalability and reliability can increase due to the highly dynamic environment, and fog computing can help decrease data traffic to the cloud.

Nevertheless, novel techniques and new approaches for modeling are required for its (network-aware) application in the context of IoE, as many devices have to become interconnected. Moreover, proper security and privacy-preserving mechanisms are necessary for its realization to avoid attacks and other security threats. The following studies illustrate the state-of-the-art challenges that are subject to research in the context of IoT and IoE models and architectures:

- Al-Janabi [3] describes a newly designed model which reduces both time and effort for students attending a lecture by using intelligent data analysis (IDA) and students' IoT devices.
- Mohsin et al. [36] focus on mutual authentication of IoT devices. They propose a comprehensive survey of current RFID systems with mutual authentification protocols with their strengths and weaknesses.
- Shamshirband and Soleimani [47] address the demand for efficient searching algorithms in peer-to-peer networks where there is no control over the object locations. They show the learning automata adaptive probabilistic search algorithm's superiority concerning its success rate with significantly reducing messages.

- Mishra and Jain [33] suggest ontologies as a semantic model for IoT-based devices and their representation of knowledge. The paper evaluates ontologies through several different metrics and presents pitfalls.

  Similarly, the following research affects IoE performance issues.

- Mishra et al. [34] address security issues for IoT networks and data transfer, such as authentification, encryption, and cyber-attacks. The paper reviews various swarm-based anomaly detection methods and evaluates them.
- Jafari et al. [22] propose and validate a method for optimized energy consumption in wireless sensor networks by using a density-based clustering algorithm. The new approach derives from the OPTICS density-based clustering environment and excels at performance compared to similar algorithms.
- Venkatesvara et al. [53] introduce a hybrid texture features extraction method that is applied to the data transfer between edge/vehicular devices to estimate a video's motion. As a result, it is possible to reduce the storage capacities required for real-time video processing.
- Okafor et al. [42] investigate the Smart Hierarchical Network in the context of IoT, as it is considered a reliable Fog dynamic design structure based on a Software Defined Artificial Neural Network. The results encourage high scalability for networks with massive computational/traffic workload requirements.

Further research related to IoE concerns the investigation of connectivity linking sensors and control systems required to connect smart things and users. Technological developments will help the IoE to strive, especially concerning artificial intelligence [45], neural networks, big data [16], semantic interoperability and data management, localization and tracking capabilities, embedded security and privacy-preserving mechanisms [30], distributed technologies such as blockchain [5], interconnectivity [7], and so much more [12].

5   An Author Vision for IoE Education

The emergence of the Internet of Everything leads to a computing education question: Should there be a curriculum surrounding IoE? We have already seen that the concept of IoT started in the 1980s, but curricula and related degree programs began around the mid-2000s, with baccalaureate degrees awarded in the 2010s, specifically in China. Hence, it has taken about twenty years (a generation) for IoT to become a computing discipline. The authors see a similar emergence developing with IoE. Namely, the concept began in the late 1990s, so we expect an IoE discipline to emerge later in the 2020s.

5.1   The Meaning of Competency

If an IoE education discipline did emerge, what might it be? We can speculate many possibilities, from ubiquitous computing to other generalized forms. It should be clear that if indeed an IoE computing education discipline became a reality, it would have to reflect the needs of its stakeholders – mainly the computing industry. The IoE curriculum should focus on competency in this situation, as promoted in the CC2020 report [13]. The CC2020 competency definition evolved from many models and definitions. Specifically, the IT2017 report [46] and the CC2020 report [13] have promoted that knowledge, skills, and dispositions (behaviors) form a cluster described as

$$\text{Competency} = \text{Knowledge} + \text{Skills} + \text{Dispositions}$$

taken in context to accomplish a task. Figure 3 is an illustration of this concept, as shown in the CC2020 report.

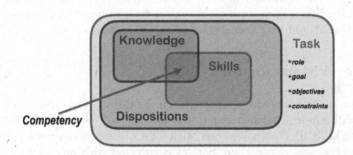

Fig. 3. Illustration of Competency [13].

We can think of *Knowledge* as the "know-what" dimension, an essential core concept for competency. The *Skills* element expresses the "know-how" dimension of competency, while the *Dispositions* frame the "know-why" dimension, suggesting a requisite characteristic in performing a task. Current teachers of computing programs at universities are experts in conveying knowledge to students. Some are also good at teaching computing skills. However, it remains questionable whether computing instructors can teach a disposition if it is some innate part of a person's character [14]. Perhaps dispositions are only an inherent outcome desired by employers. Irrespective of its current state, dispositions become a dimension of competency [44,56], the link between education and the practical world.

5.2   IoE Education

For an Internet of Everything curriculum to be successful, it must focus upon competency-based learning so that the curriculum links with the needs of its stakeholders, namely industry practitioners, educational authorities (e.g., ministries, governing bodies), computing educators, and students. Specifically, computing educators should understand how their current curriculum and a prospective IoE curriculum connect with the stakeholders. Likewise, the stakeholders should have their obligations to explore the potentially rich IoE curriculum and assist in shaping its structure so that IoE competent graduates can find a home in the workplace or delve further into advanced studies. Industry can foster active "partnerships" through meaningful internships and advisory board participation.

The Internet of Everything offers a unique opportunity to create a vibrant curriculum to address the computing curriculum-industry skills gap. The nascent nature of IoE allows it to be flexible in its curriculum development, unaffected by previous norms and faculty biases. The situation presents new horizons covering anticipated needs through a stakeholder partnership with global benefits through competency-based learning. Stakeholders should encourage computing programs to consider IoE education and establish a wholesome environment in this new learning area. IoE stakeholders must become inventive in contributing to this new horizon where competencies are central to learning. Using competency in IoE education should be a cornerstone of this new endeavor.

6   Other Visions for IoE

This section outlines several perspectives on the future of the IoE. Even though the field still requires much research, the majority of visions for a future with IoE are bright [8,10,17,35]. We start with CISCO's business-driven perspective on new markets and value. Then, Sandra Khvoynitskaya's reflection on security concerns and factors driving the IoE development and Tom Moran's extensive vision of the IoE offer other perspectives.

6.1   Market Perspective

In the business context, the CISCO white papers of 2013 and 2014 are straightforward [8,10,17,35]. They promise newly emerging market and business models for IoE. Above all, they imply huge monetary benefits for investing in transformational processes. In 2013, Bradley et al. [10] assumed a 14 trillion US$ value in the IoE, as costs can decrease while revenues are increasing. This situation is due to increased productivity of employees, a more efficient supply chain and logistics, more customers, and a high degree of innovation, causing a reduced time to market.

In 2014, Barbier et al. [8] claimed a 19 trillion US$ total value opportunity in the private sector for the following decade while expecting 50 billion connected devices in 2020. At the same time, they promote the more "efficient" exploitation of fossil fuels, oil and gas reserves through the IoE [8]. This condition seems particularly important as the world population is on the increase, more likely to live in big cities and therefore causing a lot of pressure on the energy market. So, Evans' early claims concerning humanity's benefits and counteracting climate change with the help of IoE must be questioned [17]. The same is true for the propositions by Mitchell et al. [35] regarding the improved livability in cities as a result of the IoE technology. Connected utilities and smartly monitored transportation systems certainly offer both value and opportunity for the global population [8]. The source of energy, however, is a critical aspect.

In 2020, the IoE market's value worldwide was estimated at 928.11 billion US\$ [4]. Unfortunately, verifying these numbers is impossible within the scope of this paper. Nonetheless, recent predictions reveal that the IoE market expects to reach 4,205.5 billion US\$ by 2030 at an annual growth rate of 16.5 % from 2021 to 2030 [4]. These trends in the IoE market are due to increasing urbanization, IoE software, and the internet's ubiquity, especially in North America.

6.2   Khvoynitskaya's Perspective

Sandra Khvoynitskaya presents another perspective as she discusses the expected merge of the IoE with other technologies, such as virtual and augmented reality, big data, AI, cloud computing, blockchain, and others [25]. Furthermore, the link to AI and machine learning strengthens in this context, as devices expect to become smarter and more autonomous by learning from users' patterns. This assumption reflects IoE's holistic nature and connections to several other subject areas. Furthermore, Khvoynitskaya assumes that the IoE will become more industry-specific, and new cross-industry technologies will develop (e.g., smart agriculture, smart retail, the Internet of Medical Things, etc.).

Khvoynitskaya outlines several security concerns she perceives as blind spots in the future. These comprise integration difficulties, unclear return on investment, lack of expertise to implement technology, interoperability concerns, data portability and ownership, vendor sustainability, transition risks, legal and compliance barriers, and network and vendor lock-in concerns. Nonetheless, the IoE development should strive due to falling costs for sensors, data gathering, and storage due to cloud solutions, expansion of internet connectivity, as well as an increasing number of mobile devices and computational resources [25].

6.3   Moran's Perspective

In a 2021 Tedx Talk, Tom Moran [37] presents a significant number of opportunities and developments for humans by using the IoE, thereby reflecting Dave Evans's early expectations [17]. The real power of the IoE is what Moran refers to as the "hive mind", the AI analyzing and "learning" from the gathered data. He considers the IoE the next evolutionary step, where even walls, pipes, and radiators become smart by utilizing nanotechnology. Moran includes people in this vision, as they may use smart wearables (e.g., contact lenses or augmented reality glasses) to interact with the AI or connect it to minds by some interface. Eventually, homes may become smart, alert people before a pipe breaks, or even call a plumber without inhabitants knowing or being home, or having to utter questions and needs [37]. The idea of the "big mother" taking care of our medical, mental and social activities and demands accompanies a vision of zero-emission homes, smart streets, neighborhoods, smart cities, and mega cities. According to Moran, scaling up IoE can lead to new growth and a new type of self-sustained civilization able to control emissions, electricity, farming, waste, water, traffic, and more. In other words: an intelligent world with complete control over humanity and nature. The smart solar system could be next [37].

If we continue Moran's purely capitalist narrative of infinite growth, the question arises whether the system would eventually end itself. Would humanity still strive for growth beyond the frontiers of space if everybody is taken care of by IoE? Will nature even survive the exploitation required for constructing the IoE? Will we survive in a world that will soon be hotter than ever by 2100? What happens to governments, lawmakers, and religious leaders? Will they accept the loss of power to the hive brain?

7   Conclusion

This paper addressed several perspectives on the Internet of Everything through historical pathways that led to one or more visions of its future. The IoE is a superset of IoT, which is a machine-to-machine phenomenon. However, IoE is much more than that. In addition to machine-to-machine experiences, IoE addresses the people-to-machine and the people-to-people incidents involving data and processes in an internet environment. IoE visions support this concept. The future of IoE education should encompass competency-based learning, which was the foundation of the CC2020 project and its report. The dispositions and skills dimensions of competency form the "people" part of IoE education. A competency-based framework of IoE education would ensure its success.

A realistic vision for the Internet of Everything should increase the understanding of a world that can strive for increased innovation in the future. Moreover, IoE can provide the groundwork for solving complex computing issues. One of the main questions is whether people desire to become transparent users by sharing all data and giving up control. Are we ready to do that? If so, who will push for further innovations? How will IoE reshape today's society?

The implications of IoE certainly go well beyond current computing and computing education. Therefore, IoE will soon require intensive consideration and research from all disciplines. Whether IoE becomes "the next big thing" is hard to guess. Its future is in your hands.

References

1. Acimovic, I.: Internet of Things - past, present and the future of connected system (2020). https://itsupplychain.com/internet-of-things-past-present-the-future-of-a-connected-system/
2. Albrecht, G.: Apple enthüllt iPad (Apple Launches iPad) (2010). https://www.apple.com/de/newsroom/2010/01/27Apple-Launches-iPad/
3. Al_Janabi, S.: Smart system to create an optimal higher education environment using IDA and IOTs. Int. J. Comput. Appl. **42**(3), 244–259 (2020)
4. Allied Market Research: Internet Of Everything (IoE) Market Research, 2030 (2022). https://www.alliedmarketresearch.com/internet-of-everything-market
5. Anjum, A., Sporny, M., Sill, A.: Blockchain standards for compliance and trust. IEEE Cloud Comput. **4**(4), 84–90 (2017)

6. Ashton, K.: Internet of everything vs internet of things (2009). https://www.rfidjournal.com/that-internet-of-things-thing

7. Azodolmolky, S., Wieder, P., Yahyapour, R.: SDN-based cloud computing networking. In: 2013 15th International Conference on Transparent Optical Networks (ICTON), pp. 1–4. IEEE (2013)

8. Barbier, J., Bhatia, P.K., Kapoor, D.: Internet of Everything in ASEAN driving value and opportunity in oil and gas, utilities, and transportation (2014). https://www.cisco.com/c/dam/en_us/about/ac79/docs/IoE/IoE-in-ASEAN.pdf

9. Barrett, M., Davidson, E., Prabhu, J., Vargo, S.L.: Service innovation in the digital age. MIS Q. **39**(1), 135–154 (2015)

10. Bradley, J., Barbier, J., Handler, D.: Embracing the Internet of everything to capture your share of 14.4 trillion: more relevant, valuable connections will improve innovation, productivity, efficiency & customer experience (2013). https://www.cisco.com/c/dam/en_us/about/ac79/docs/innov/IoE_Economy.pdf

11. Cambridge Dictionary: Internet of Things (2021). https://dictionary.cambridge.org/de/worterbuch/englisch/internet-of-things?q=Internet+of+Things

12. Cardoso, P.J., Monteiro, J., Semião, J., Rodrigues, J.M.: Harnessing the Internet of Everything (IoE) for Accelerated Innovation Opportunities. IGI Global, Pennsylvania (2019)

13. CC2020 Task Force: Computing curricula 2020 (cc2020): paradigms for future computing curricula. Technical report, Association for Computing Machinery / IEEE Computer Society, New York, NY, USA (2020). http://www.cc2020.net/

14. Clear, T.: THINKING ISSUES meeting employers expectations of devops roles: can dispositions be taught? ACM Inroads **8**(2), 19–21 (2017)

15. Farias da Costa, V.C., Oliveira, L., de Souza, J.: Internet of Everything (IoE) taxonomies: a survey and a novel knowledge-based taxonomy. Sensors **21**(2), 568 (2021)

16. Da Xu, L., He, W., Li, S.: Internet of things in industries: a survey. IEEE Trans. Industr. Inf. **10**(4), 2233–2243 (2014)

17. Evans, D.: The Internet of Everything: how more relevant and valuable connections will change the world (2012. https://www.cisco.com/c/dam/global/en_my/assets/ciscoinnovate/pdfs/IoE.pdf, cisco Internet Business Solutions Group (IBSG), Cisco Systems Inc, San Jose, USA, White Paper

18. Featherly, K.: ARPANET - United States defense program (2021). https://www.britannica.com/topic/ARPANET. encyclopedia Britannica

19. Fenn, J., LeHong, H.: Hype cycle for emerging technologies 2011 (2011). https://www.gartner.com/en/documents/1754719/hype-cycle-for-emerging-technologies-2011

20. Fredette, J., Marom, R., Steiner, K., Witters, L.: The promise and peril of hyperconnectivity for organizations and societies. Glob. Inf. Technol. Rep. **2012**, 113–119 (2012)

21. Gambardella, A., McGahan, A.M.: Business-model innovation: general purpose technologies and their implications for industry structure. Long Range Plan. **43**(2–3), 262–271 (2010)

22. Jafari, H., Nazari, M., Shamshirband, S.: Optimization of energy consumption in wireless sensor networks using density-based clustering algorithm. Int. J. Comput. Appl. **43**(1), 1–10 (2021)

23. Keen, P., Williams, R.: Value architectures for digital business: beyond the business model. MIS Q. **37**(2), 643–647 (2013)

24. Khan, S., Al Shayokh, M., Miraz, M.H., Bhuiyan, M.: A framework for android based shopping mall applications. In: Proceedings of The International Conference on eBusiness, eCommerce, eManagement, eLearning and eGovernance 2014: IC5E 2014, vol. 1, p. 12181. Association of Scientists, Developers and Faculties (2013)
25. Khvoynitskaya, S.: The IoT history and future (2019). https://www.itransition.com/blog/iot-history
26. Langley, D.J., van Doorn, J., Ng, I.C., Stieglitz, S., Lazovik, A., Boonstra, A.: The Internet of Everything: amart things and their impact on business models. J. Bus. Res. **122**, 853–863 (2021)
27. Marinova, D., de Ruyter, K., Huang, M.H., Meuter, M.L., Challagalla, G.: Getting smart: learning from technology-empowered frontline interactions. J. Serv. Res. **20**(1), 29–42 (2017)
28. Massa, L., Tucci, C.L., Afuah, A.: A critical assessment of business model research. Acad. Manag. Ann. **11**(1), 73–104 (2017)
29. Merriam-Webster Dictionary: Internet of Things (2021). https://www.merriam-webster.com/dictionary/InternetofThings
30. Miorandi, D., Sicari, S., De Pellegrini, F., Chlamtac, I.: Internet of things: vision, applications and research challenges. Ad Hoc Netw. **10**(7), 1497–1516 (2012)
31. Miraz, M.H., Ali, M., Excell, P.S., Picking, R.: A review on internet of things (IoT), internet of everything (IoE) and internet of nano things (IoNT). In: 2015 Internet Technologies and Applications (ITA), pp. 219–224. IEEE (2015)
32. Miraz, M.H., Khan, S., Bhuiyan, M., Excell, P.S.: Mobile academy: A ubiquitous mobile learning (mLearning) platform. In: Proceedings of the International Conference on eBusiness, eCommerce, eManagement, eLearning and eGovernance (IC5E 2014), held at University of Greenwich, London, UK, pp. 89–95 (2014)
33. Mishra, S., Jain, S.: Ontologies as a semantic model in IoT. Int. J. Comput. Appl. **42**(3), 233–243 (2020)
34. Mishra, S., Sagban, R., Yakoob, A., Gandhi, N.: Swarm intelligence in anomaly detection systems: an overview. Int. J. Comput. Appl. **43**(2), 109–118 (2021)
35. Mitchell, S., Villa, N., Stewart-Weeks, M., Lange, A.: The Internet of Everything for Cities Connecting People, Process, Data, and Things To Improve the 'Livability' of Cities and Communities (2013). https://www.cisco.com/c/dam/en_us/solutions/industries/docs/gov/everything-for-cities.pdf
36. Mohsin, S.M., Khan, I.A., Abrar Akber, S.M., Shamshirband, S., Chronopoulos, A.T.: Exploring the RFID mutual authentication domain. Int. J. Comput. Appl. **43**(2), 127–141 (2021)
37. Moran, T.: The Internet of Everything. Online video presentation TEDx Talks (2021). https://youtu.be/K-FhMegdlJo
38. Ng, I., Scharf, K., Pogrebna, G., Maull, R.: Contextual variety, Internet-of-Things and the choice of tailoring over platform: mass customisation strategy in supply chain management. Int. J. Prod. Econ. **159**, 76–87 (2015)
39. Ng, I., Wakenshaw, S.: Service ecosystems: a timely worldview for a connected, digital and data-driven economy, The Sage Handbook of Service-Dominant Logic, pp. 199–213. Sage, London (2018)
40. Ng, I.C.: Creating New Markets in the Digital Economy. Cambridge University Press, Cambridge (2014)
41. Ng, I.C., Vargo, S.L.: Service-dominant (SD) logic, service ecosystems and institutions: bridging theory and practice. J. Serv. Manag. **29**(4), 518–520 (2018)
42. Okafor, K., Ononiwu, G., Goundar, S., Chijindu, V., Udeze, C.: Towards complex dynamic fog network orchestration using embedded neural switch. Int. J. Comput. Appl. **43**(2), 91–108 (2021)

43. Oryema, B., Kim, H.S., Li, W., Park, J.T.: Design and implementation of an inter-operable messaging system for IoT healthcare services. In: 2017 14th IEEE Annual Consumer Communications Networking Conference (CCNC), pp. 45–52 (2017)

44. Raj, R., et al.: Professional competencies in computing education: pedagogies and assessment. In: Proceedings of the 2021 Working Group Reports on Innovation and Technology in Computer Science Education, pp. 133–161. ITiCSE-WGR 2021, ACM, New York, USA (2021). https://doi.org/10.1145/3502870.3506570

45. Russell, S., Norvig, P.: Artificial Intelligence: A Modern Approach (2002)

46. Sabin, M., et al.: Information Technology Curricula 2017 (IT2017). ACM/IEEE Computer Society, New York, NY, USA, Technical report (2017)

47. Shamshirband, S., Soleimani, H.: LAAPS: an efficient file-based search in unstructured peer-to-peer networks using reinforcement algorithm. Int. J. Comput. Appl. **43**(1), 62–69 (2021)

48. Shinkarenko, A.: Internet of Everything vs Internet of Things (2020). https://www.itransition.com/blog/internet-of-everything-vs-internet-of-things

49. Shojafar, M., Sookhak, M.: Internet of everything, networks, applications, and computing systems (IoENACS). Int. J. Comput. Appl. **42**(3), 213–215 (2020)

50. Teece, D.J.: Dynamic capabilities: routines versus entrepreneurial action. J. Manage. Stud. **49**(8), 1395–1401 (2012)

51. Teicher, J.: The little-known story of the first IoT device (2018). https://www.ibm.com/blogs/industries/little-known-story-first-iot-device/

52. Turber, S., vom Brocke, J., Gassmann, O., Fleisch, E.: Designing business models in the era of internet of things. In: Tremblay, M.C., VanderMeer, D., Rothenberger, M., Gupta, A., Yoon, V. (eds.) DESRIST 2014. LNCS, vol. 8463, pp. 17–31. Springer, Cham (2014). https://doi.org/10.1007/978-3-319-06701-8_2

53. Venkatesvara Rao, N., Venkatavara Prasad, D., Sugumaran, M.: Real-time video object detection and classification using hybrid texture feature extraction. Int. J. Comput. Appl. **43**(2), 119–126 (2021)

54. Weissberger, A.: TiECon 2014 Summary-Part 1: Qualcomm Keynote & IoT Track Overview (2014). https://techblog.comsoc.org/2014/05/23/tiecon-2014-summary-part-1-qualcomm-keynote-iot-track-overview/. iEEE ComSoc

55. Westerlund, M., Leminen, S., Rajahonka, M.: Designing business models for the internet of things. Technol. Innov. Manag. Rev. 5–14 (2014)

56. Impagliazzo, J., Kiesler, N., Kumar, A.N., Mackellar, B., Raj, R.K., Sabin, M.: Perspectives on dispositions in computing competencies. In: Proceedings of the 27th ACM Conference on on Innovation and Technology in Computer Science Education, ITiCSE'22, Dublin, Ireland, vol. 2, pp. 662–663 (2022). https://doi.org/10.1145/3502717.3532121

Guidelines to Develop Consumers Cyber Resilience Capabilities in the IoE Ecosystem

Eliana Stavrou[✉] [iD]

Faculty of Pure and Applied Sciences, Open University of Cyprus, Nicosia, Cyprus
eliana.stavrou@ouc.ac.cy

Abstract. The IoE ecosystem presents ongoing cybersecurity challenges that need to be addressed by all actors to effectively defend against the dynamics of the relevant cyber threat landscape. The consumer IoT market constitutes a key element of the IoE ecosystem that must be protected from cyber criminals. To effectively defend against cybercriminals, consumers must adopt a more active role and become more resilient to attacks. This means that they need to be able to proactively anticipate attacks, defend and effectively respond to a security incident. To this end, it is essential to promote the development of basic technical skills to a level appropriate for consumers. This is an important aspect that should drive the design of specialized cybersecurity curricula in the context of the IoE ecosystem. This research work provides guidelines to curricula designers and trainers as to the thematic areas they should consider in the design and delivery of specialized cybersecurity curricula to build consumers' cyber resilience competencies in the context of the IoE ecosystem. For each thematic area, the key topics to consider in the design of the curricula are specified, highlighting specific skills and knowledge that should be developed. The design of such curricula can contribute in upskilling consumers and improving the cyber resilience level across society.

Keywords: Cyber resilience · Cyber hygiene · Consumer IoT · Cybersecurity education · Societal cyber resilience

1 Introduction

The digital transformation that was observed across the globe as an outcome of the impact caused by the COVID-19 pandemic, has forced citizens to utilize a range of smart products and use technologies without realizing the potential threat they bring in their homes [1]. These smart connected products are often referred to as the Internet of Things (IoT), which is part of a greater concept, that of the Internet of Everything (IoE). IoE is a complete ecosystem that consists of four key elements: things, people, data, and processes, where the Internet forms the foundation of these elements. According to [2], the number of IoT devices worldwide is forecast to almost triple from 8.74 billion in 2020 to more than 25.4 billion IoT devices in 2030. By 2030, it is anticipated that around 60% of all IoT connected devices will concern the consumer sector.

T. Pereira et al. (Eds.): IoECon 2022, LNICST 458, pp. 18–28, 2023.
https://doi.org/10.1007/978-3-031-25222-8_2

IoT products have become part of everyday life as consumers have realized the great benefits of using these products, such as convenience and personalization. The utilization of IoT devices can assist in saving valuable time in an era of fast-paced world, which can be dedicated to other essential aspects of consumers' life such as family and wellbeing.

Although IoT devices have many benefits, it is well known that they constitute crown jewels for cybercriminals who continue to exploit a range of well-known vulnerabilities, such as insecure passwords, insecure ecosystem interfaces, outdated components and unencrypted communications [3]. According to Netscout Systems [4], the average IoT device gets attacked just five minutes after it goes online. Unfortunately, this trend will get worst as more devices get connected and extend the overall IoE attack surface. As indicated in the survey performed by the Consumers International and the Internet Society [5], approximately 50% of the survey's participants reported distrusting their connected devices to protect their privacy and handle their information in a respectful manner. Even though the low trust levels to connected IoT devices, consumers still use them due to the benefits they offer.

The IoE ecosystem presents ongoing cybersecurity challenges that need to be addressed to defend against the dynamics of the cyber threat landscape. To increase the chances to effectively defend against cybercriminals and become more cyber resilient, consumers must adopt a more active role and support the efforts to protect the IoE ecosystem. The plug-and-play nature of the IoT devices, alongside the utilization of a range of IoT-powered applications makes the whole experience transparent to consumers who often do not realize the technologies they use and the relevant risk, or it's magnitude, for their privacy and safety and how this can extend and impact the entire society. It is imperative to upskill consumers on fundamental cybersecurity aspects and make them aware of the situation in cyber space. Currently, cybersecurity awareness raising efforts have not achieved the appropriate level of competencies among consumers [6]. To start building consumers' cyber resilience capabilities, curricula designers should consider building capabilities across the five functional cybersecurity areas (identify, protect, detect, respond, and recover) specified in NIST Cybersecurity Framework [7].

This research work targets to highlight the urgency to educate consumers, beyond awareness raising, and build their cyber resilience competencies so they demonstrate a responsible behavior as actors in the IoE ecosystem. In the context of this work, guidelines to curricula designers and trainers are provided, as to the thematic areas they need to consider when developing and delivering specialized cybersecurity curricula for consumers in the context of the IoE.

Section 2 presents existing work. Section 3 discusses societal cyber resilience competencies in the context of IoE and Sect. 4 presents the thematic areas to consider in the design of specialized curricula to build consumers' cyber resilience skills and knowledge in the context of the IoE ecosystem. Finally, Sect. 5 concludes this research work.

2   Literature Review

For the past decade, the cybersecurity community's efforts converged towards raising awareness across society on fundamental cybersecurity aspects. A key aspect of all these efforts was to build a societal cyber hygiene culture [8, 9] and defend against the dynamics of the cyber threat landscape. The most recent example of COVID-19 pandemic, demonstrated how fast the cyber threat landscape [10] can be transformed and expand its attack surface across society. The pandemic forced citizens to adapt their lifestyle and habits to cope with lock downs, work from home, socialize and maintain their wellbeing. Inevitable, the rapid digital transformation that occurred across society to address the pandemic's impact, also forced the adoption of more connected devices in consumers' homes. According to [11], the average UK consumer utilizes more than nine connected devices. Another study [12] highlights how COVID-19 impacted consumers, highlighting that consumers are utilizing more connected devices than at the start of the pandemic. The average U.S. household now utilizes 25 connected devices. This means that the attack surface is expanded as consumers connect more products to create smarter homes.

The rising use of IoT consumer devices in recent years, attracted the attention of cybercriminals, especially due to the poor security protection that many of these devices offer [1, 13]. OWASP Top 10 IoT 2018 list [3] is highlighting ten IoT-related vulnerabilities, including insecure passwords, insecure ecosystem interfaces and outdated components. Cybercriminals demonstrated their ability to build massive botnets from compromised IoT devices and launch Distributed Denial of Service (DDoS) attacks or distribute malware [10]. A recent example is Mirai malware [14], that targeted primarily IoT consumer devices, such as IP cameras and routers, and turned them into remotely controlled bots utilized in DDoS attacks against major internet platforms and services.

The necessity of developing a cyber hygiene culture [8, 9] is stronger than ever. This includes being aware of best cybersecurity practices and apply them to stay secure in cyberspace. To this end, the cybersecurity community has been delivering cybersecurity education courses and awareness raising activities across society. These activities have been developed taking into consideration different cybersecurity curricula guidelines and frameworks, such as the CSE2017 [15] and the CyBOK [16]. The focus of these guidelines has been primarily to highlight the knowledge that needs to be developed across different areas in cybersecurity. This approach has been reflected in the design of many cybersecurity education and awareness raising activities delivered across society.

Cybersecurity awareness raising campaigns often include the delivery of presentations, promotion of infographics, posters, guides, and tips on how to stay secure in cyberspace, e.g., [12]. An overall observation is that these resources are often passively delivered to the target audience. More engaging activities are also delivered by national authorities, academia, and private sector, focusing on younger people. Such activities include participation in cyber competitions, boot camps, and cyber computer games, e.g., [14–16].

Even though the cyber awareness raising efforts, these have not been very effective to reach a satisfactory societal cyber resilience level. This is due to different factors as indicated by existing studies, e.g., [17, 18]. Users often prefer convenience over security, and they demonstrate an online behavior that in several cases is associated with bad cyber practices. The studies have also shown that people often do not demonstrate a cyber hygiene behavior simply because they are not aware of the situation, they lack understanding of the relevant concepts, or they do not know how to apply a security measure [19].

To address the dynamics in the cyber threat landscape, consumers need to become more resilient to attacks, which means they need to be able to proactively anticipate attacks, defend and effectively respond to a security incident. The need to build societal cyber resilience competencies has been highlighted in many studies, e.g. [6, 20–23]. When considering consumers, it is obvious that the expectations should not be the same as when dealing with professionals, but nonetheless it is essential to build some basic technical competencies to the level appropriate for consumers. This is an important aspect that should drive the design of specialized cybersecurity curricula in the context of the IoE ecosystem.

3 Societal Cyber Resilience Competencies

According to the National Institute of Standards and Technology (NIST), cyber resiliency is "the ability to anticipate, withstand, recover from, and adapt to adverse conditions, stresses, attacks, or compromises on systems that use or are enabled by cyber resources." Currently, cybersecurity awareness raising efforts focused on developing fundamental knowledge on cybersecurity aspects. This approach may have increased to some level the understanding of consumers of the importance of cybersecurity but has not been that effective in convincing people to change their behavior and adopt a responsible cyber hygiene behavior. This might be because cybersecurity awareness raising efforts have not focused on developing the practical skills of consumers so they can actually apply best cybersecurity practices [6]. Thus, we need to rewire the approach we take when designing and developing cybersecurity awareness raising activities and integrate more practical aspects, such as demonstrations and hands-on activities, to promote the development of critical thinking skills. By adopting a what-if-how philosophy, consumers can start building the necessary skills and knowledge to effectively address a cyber threat. Currently, consumers capabilities are not developed to an adequate level, and this is evident from the recent cyber statistics related to COVID-19, that demonstrated that incidents have exponentially increased, leading to data breaches across the society.

To effectively deal with the dynamics of the cyber threat landscape, efforts have focus on building a cybersecurity capacity. As per ENISA guidelines, many countries have specified their national cybersecurity strategy, including objectives to build a cybersecurity culture and relevant capabilities across society [24], considering children, young adults, seniors, the workforce, etc. In this context, authorities tasked with the supervision and implementation of the national cybersecurity strategies, should consider the necessity to upskill consumers and build relevant knowledge and skills to utilize IoT devices in a secure manner. The effort to build an IoT-focused cybersecurity culture should start from a young age, as young people will constitute the future citizens as soon as they enter adulthood. The necessity to develop a minimum exposure to cybersecurity across a global community, starting from a young age, is also highlighted in [25]. To develop a strong educated global community against IoT cyber threats, it is equally important to design appropriate curricula in higher education and adult education so that young people and adults can be educated on the cyber threats that are relevant to IoT and build skills to address them effectively. Therefore, national authorities should coordinate efforts to bring appropriate stakeholders together to collectively work on building appropriate capabilities. Depending on the audience, their skills and learning objectives, the appropriate learning material and pedagogies need to be developed. It is envisioned that this work can serve as a basis to guide curricula designers as to the thematic areas they need to first consider and initiate further investigations to support the development of a cybersecurity capacity.

To start building consumers' cyber resilience, curricula designers should consider building consumers' competencies across the NIST Cybersecurity Framework areas [7]: identify, protect, detect, respond, and recover. Thematic areas should be specified within the context of the NIST Cybersecurity Framework to build capabilities across all the functional cybersecurity areas. In the context of the identify area, efforts should focus on building consumers' understanding of the fundamentals related to the IoT ecosystem, identify its components and their value on a personal and societal level. At the same time, consumers need to realize the dynamics of the cyber threat landscape, how specific cyberattacks can be delivered and the impact that might arise on a personal and societal level if an attack is successful. To this end, a key aspect is to highlight the adversaries' mindset and the techniques they utilize so that citizens are aware of the situation, realize the adversarial capabilities and how realistic a compromisation can be. In terms of protection, knowledge and skills should be developed related to choosing and applying best practices and solutions so consumers can proactively address cyber threats and minimize the risk of getting compromised. The next area covers detection aspects. Appropriate capabilities need to be developed so that consumers can identify signs of infection which can trigger them to apply response and recovery actions to limit the impact from a potential cyber incident. Such actions may entail communicating the incident to appropriate authorities, reconfiguring tools, using other mitigation actions to effectively manage the security incident, etc. Table 1 presents the thematic areas that are derived taking into consideration the NIST Cybersecurity Framework and the IoT-related cyber threat landscape [3, 10]. The proposed thematic areas (TA) are specified across 8 topics: TA1 IoE Fundamentals, TA2 Cyber threats, TA3 Social Engineering Attacks, TA4 Authentication Controls, TA5 Software Patches & Updates, TA6 Malware Defenses, TA7 Secure Communications & Data Security, and TA8 Incident Handling and Response. Section 4 discusses in detail the proposed thematic areas.

Figure 1 lists the thematic areas included in Table 1, the relevant high-level learning objectives that should be pursued in the context of the five cybersecurity areas (identify, protect, detect, respond, and recover) and maps them to the Bloom's taxonomy. As indicated in Fig. 1, the first three layers (remember, understand, apply) of Bloom's taxonomy can promote consumers' situational awareness. Situational awareness capabilities should be perceived as the fundamental capabilities needed towards societal cyber resilience. Once consumers acquire such capabilities, then the next step is to cultivate their critical thinking skills in the context of the other layers (analyze, evaluate, create) of the Bloom's taxonomy. By developing this skillset, consumers can take an active role in the management of cyber incidents, and a sustainable cyber hygiene behavior can be promoted.

Table 1. Thematic areas mapped to NIST Cybersecurity Framework areas

NIST Cybersecurity framework functional areas	Thematic Areas (TA)
Identify	TA1 IoE Fundamentals TA2 Cyber Threats TA3 Social engineering attacks
Protect	TA4 Authentication Controls TA5 Software Patches & Updates TA6 Malware Defenses TA7 Secure Communications & Data Security
Detect	TA 8 Incident Handling and Response
Respond	
Recover	

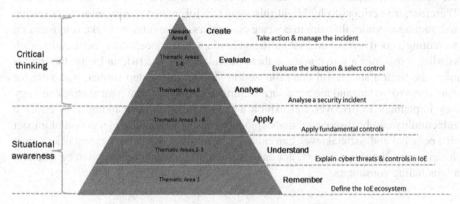

Fig. 1. Pursued high-level learning objectives versus Bloom's taxonomy

4   IoE Curricula Design Guidelines

This section provides guidelines to curricula designers and trainers as to the thematic areas they should consider in the design and delivery of specialized cybersecurity curricula to build consumers' cyber resilience competencies in the context of the IoE ecosystem. For each thematic area, the key topics to consider in the design of the curricula are specified, highlighting specific skills and knowledge that should be developed in the context of the NIST Cybersecurity Framework and taking into consideration the IoT-related cyber threat landscape [3, 10].

4.1   Thematic Area 1: IoE Fundamentals

The aim of this thematic area is to introduce to consumers the IoE ecosystem, present its characteristics and how it fits in the context of ubiquitous decentralization. Understanding the decentralized nature of this environment should be a key element of this thematic area as it is the first step to realize the cybersecurity challenges linked to this ecosystem. The IoE ecosystem extends the traditional (centralized) security perimeter which now is distributed across the IoE ecosystem. Therefore, protection needs to be applied across the different components that constitute the IoE ecosystem. An important element of the IoE ecosystem is the IoT. Consumers have a significant role in the IoE ecosystem as end-users of IoT products, e.g., in the context of smart homes. Efforts should be placed on raising awareness across consumers regarding the risks that exist in this environment so they can realize how their privacy can be compromised and take informed decisions when utilizing IoT solutions, including applying best practices to enhance their security.

4.2 Thematic Area 2: IoE Cyber Threats

A variety of cyber threats are related to IoE and need to be addressed by different actors, e.g., consumers, professionals, policy makers, etc., by applying appropriate technologies and controls. Consumers cannot defend what they do not know or do not understand. Therefore, it is critical to highlight this aspect in IoE cybersecurity awareness raising and training modules that aim to educate consumers. An approach to take is to focus on promoting a good level of understanding on fundamental concepts in cybersecurity, such as what constitutes a threat actor, a threat, a vulnerability, a risk and what the impact might be from a successful compromisation. Taking this a step further, it is vital for consumers to understand the adversaries' mindset and what is the typical attack strategy they implement to discover and exploit a vulnerability. Understanding how easily a vulnerability can be discovered and exploited, and the magnitude of a potential impact on a personal and societal level, can enhance the concept that cybersecurity is an aspect that concerns the entire society, not only professionals, and actions need to be taken by all, including consumers.

4.3 Thematic Area 3: Social Engineering Attacks

Even though the efforts of the cybersecurity community to increase awareness on social engineering attacks, a great percentage of consumers still falls for the phish. As IoE evolves and consumers are presented with new smart solutions, they need to be equipped with the necessary knowledge and skills to identify the different forms of social engineering, e.g., phishing, vishing, etc., and defend accordingly by applying critical thinking and taking smart decisions. The fact that adversaries often profile their targets to increase the success of a social engineering attack, is not usually evident to consumers. Thus, it is important to highlight this aspect in cyber raising awareness sessions and to build knowledge and skills to consumers to evaluate how personal and other IoE-related data can be glued together to profile someone and perform a social engineering attack. Moreover, to build societal resilience, consumers need to be able to anticipate social engineering attacks in the context of smart environments, especially in the case of smart homes. By having the ability to anticipate potential social engineering attacks, consumers might have better chances to identify and address such an attack.

4.4 Thematic Area 4: Authentication Controls

Weak authentication is a common vulnerability [1, 3] that adversaries are exploiting to gain unauthorised access to systems. The bad password construction strategies that consumers are using are well known to the adversaries. Unfortunately, consumers often do not realize that the strategies they are using lead to weak passwords. Having a false sense of security is a great obstacle to overcome and convince consumers to change their habits. To address this obstacle, one approach to consider is to demonstrate to consumers how password cracking is performed, and how the adversaries' chances to succeed increase by using bad password construction strategies or by profiling a target. In thematic area 3, the topic of profiling a user is covered. Profiling can be useful in different aspects of compromising authentication controls, such as identifying answers to authentication questions. The extent to which profiling can be utilized is usually not evident to consumers. By demonstrating how profiling can be useful to an adversary, consumers can become more reflective when sharing information and using sensor data. This thematic area should also cover other essential topics such as authentication management and develop citizens' capabilities to utilize a password manager.

4.5 Thematic Area 5: Software Patches and Updates

Use of outdated IoT components is among OWASP IoT Top 10 list [3] of vulnerabilities. Adversaries have in their arsenal a variety of tools which can utilize to scan for vulnerable devices and identify unpatched and/or outdated systems with known vulnerabilities. In the IoE ecosystem, there are different devices, e.g., smart phones, tablets, networking appliances, sensors, etc., that consumers need to keep up to date to limit the risk of exploitation. Although cybersecurity raising awareness activities highlight the need to keep systems up to date, they touch this aspect superficially rather than developing consumers' skills to be able to perform this task. Although updating components is not always straightforward and it depends on the device capabilities [13], it is essential to equip citizens with appropriate knowledge and skills to configure automatic updates where possible, and also perform manual updates where automating this task might not be supported.

4.6 Thematic Area 6: Malware Defenses

Malware is a common attack vector that adversaries are utilizing to compromise the operation of systems, exfiltrate sensitive information or perform other malicious activities. Consumers should gain a good understanding of the different types of malware, e.g., botnets, ransomware, crypto-miner, keyloggers, etc., what their purpose is and how these can be delivered to them. To protect against malware, consumers should at least know how to use an anti-malware solution which they need to keep up to date. Furthermore, appropriate skills should be developed to be able to configure devices, e.g., smartphone, tablet, etc., to conduct an automated or manual anti-malware scan.

4.7 Thematic Area 7: Secure Communications and Data Security

An essential security property is confidentiality. Confidentiality ensures that the data are kept secret from third parties that are not authorized to access them. Data confidentiality must be protected either while data are in transit, meaning they are communicated between actors and/or devices in the IoE ecosystem, or they are at rest. Consumers should be educated on the available encryption standards and tools to use to secure communications and protect data stored on the IoE devices. Building such knowledge can support consumers in making informed decisions when having to select appropriate security configurations and protect their data. Moreover, given that wireless and cellular networks are a core component of the IoE ecosystem, consumers should develop capabilities to configure, for example, wireless access points, wireless routers, and mobile devices to use the strongest encryption standards possible.

Data at rest should also be protected. Thus, citizens should be able to use encryption tools and/or configure IoE devices and platforms to encrypt sensitive information stored on them.

4.8 Thematic Area 8: Incident Handling and Response

Building citizens' knowledge and skills on incident handling and response can tremendously support the efforts to promote societal cyber resilience. By having consumers reporting potential cyber incidents, authorities can take early actions to launch specialized awareness raising campaigns, issue guidelines, etc., and proactively prepare consumers for malicious activities that might be rising. As a first step, it is essential to guide consumers to maintain contact information of appropriate security authorities which they can contact to report an incident. Beyond that, it is a necessity to build capabilities so that consumers can identify abnormal behavior of an IoE device. To this end, curriculum designers should consider what abnormal behavior entails at a level that consumers can understand and identify. It should not be assumed that consumers have deep technical knowledge and capabilities to perform deep investigations regarding an incident. At the very least, consumers should be able to interpret results from tools such as anti-malware tools and be aware of the situation.

Once the fundamental capabilities are developed across the thematic areas presented in this work, then the next step is to specify more advanced topics to deepen consumers' knowledge and skills.

5 Conclusions

The IoE brings together people, processes, data, and things to create smarter environments across different sectors. In the context of consumer IoE ecosystem, connected devices in households provide new capabilities, richer experiences and offer a better quality of services and life to citizens. Even though the benefits, connected devices pose a great risk to consumers if a cyber hygiene behavior is not adopted. Consumers constitute a key actor in the IoE ecosystem. Efforts should be made to educate consumers, beyond cybersecurity awareness raising, to build their cyber resilience competencies.

Such competencies will allow consumers to protect their connected devices and data and handle a potential incident to a reasonable level. It is time to start specifying the fundamental technical skills that consumers need to acquire and design specialized curricula to develop them. The aim of this research work was to identify the thematic areas in which cyber resilience competencies should be developed and provide initial directions to curricula designers and trainers as to the key topics they need to consider when designing and delivering specialized curricula in the context of the IoE ecosystem. Future work will extend the current contributions, providing further guidelines, specifying the learning objectives and the pedagogy to materialize a relevant cybersecurity curriculum and upskill consumers, aiming to increase societal cyber resilience in the context of the IoE ecosystem.

References

1. Malan, J., Eager, J., Lale-Demoz, E., Cacciaguerra, G., Brady, M.: Framing the Nature and Scale of Cyber Security Vulnerabilities within the Current Consumer Internet of Things (IoT) Landscape. Centre for Strategy & Evaluation (2020)
2. Holst, A.: 'IoT connected devices worldwide 2019–2030', *Statista*. https://www.statista.com/statistics/1183457/iot-connected-devices-worldwide/. Accessed 13 Dec 2021
3. OWASP, OWASP Internet of Things Project. https://wiki.owasp.org/index.php/OWASP_Internet_of_Things_Project#tab=Main. Accessed 14 Dec 14 2021
4. NETSCOUT, Threat Intelligence Report - Dawn of the Terrorbit Era. Accessed 13 Dec 2021. https://www.netscout.com/sites/default/files/2019-02/SECR_001_EN-1901%20-%20NETSCOUT%20Threat%20Intelligence%20Report%202H%202018.pdf
5. Internet Society, The Trust Opportunity: Exploring Consumer Attitudes to the Internet of Things, *Internet Society*. https://www.internetsociety.org/resources/doc/2019/trust-opportunity-exploring-consumer-attitudes-to-iot/. Accessed 13 Dec 2021
6. Stavrou, E.: Back to basics: towards building societal resilience against a cyber pandemic. J. Systemics, Cybern. Inf. **18**(7), 73–80 (2020)
7. NIST, NIST Cybersecurity Framework, *NIST*, February 05, 2018. https://www.nist.gov/cyberframework/framework. Accessed 30 May 2022
8. Maennel, K., Mäses, S., Maennel, O.: Cyber hygiene: the big picture. In: Gruschka, N. (ed.) NordSec 2018. LNCS, vol. 11252, pp. 291–305. Springer, Cham (2018). https://doi.org/10.1007/978-3-030-03638-6_18
9. Vishwanath, A., et al.: Cyber hygiene: The concept, its measure, and its initial tests. Decis. Support Syst. **128**, 113160 (2020). https://doi.org/10.1016/j.dss.2019.113160
10. ENISA, ENISA Threat Landscape 2021, *ENISA*. https://www.enisa.europa.eu/publications/enisa-threat-landscape-2021. Accessed 14 Dec 2021
11. Vailshery, L., Sujay.: Average number of connected devices in UK households 2020. *Statista*. https://www.statista.com/statistics/1107269/average-number-connected-devices-uk-house/. Accessed 14 Dec 2021
12. Deloitte, How the pandemic has stress-tested the crowded digital home. https://www2.deloitte.com/us/en/insights/industry/telecommunications/connectivity-mobile-trends-survey.html. Accessed 13 Dec 2021
13. ENISA, Guidelines for Securing the Internet of Things, *ENISA*. https://www.enisa.europa.eu/publications/guidelines-for-securing-the-internet-of-things. Accessed 14 Dec 2021
14. Wikipedia, 'Mirai (malware)', *Wikipedia*. December. 14, 2021. https://en.wikipedia.org/w/index.php?title=Mirai(malware)&oldid=1060214070. Accessed 14 Dec 2021

15. Joint Task Force on Cybersecurity E, Cybersecurity Curricula 2017. New York NY, USA: ACM 2018 https://doi.org/10.1145/3422808

16. 'CyBOK', *The Cyber Security Body Of Knowledge*. https://www.cybok.org/. Accessed 30 May 2022

17. Bada, M., Sasse, A.M., Nurse, J.R.C.: Cyber security awareness campaigns: why do they fail to change behaviour? In: Proceedings of the International Conference on Cyber Security for Sustainable Society (CSSS, 2015), pp. 118–131 Coventry, UK (2015)

18. Goel, S., Williams, K., Dincelli, E.: Got phished? internet security and human vulnerability. J. Assoc. Inf. Syst. **18**, 22–44 (2017). https://doi.org/10.17705/1jais.00447

19. ENISA, Cybersecurity Culture Guidelines: Behavioural Aspects of Cybersecurity, April 16, 2019. https://www.enisa.europa.eu/publications/cybersecurity-culture-guidelines-behavioural-aspects-of-cybersecurity. Accessed 14 Dec 2021

20. European Commission, Joint Research Centre, Baldini, G., Barrero, J., Draper, G., et al.: Cybersecurity, our digital anchor : a European perspective. In: Dewar, M., et al. (eds.) Publications Office (2020). https://data.europa.eu/doi/10.2760/352218. Accessed 14 Dec 14 2021

21. McCormac, A., Calic, D., Parsons, K., Butavicius, M., Pattinson, M., Lillie, M.: The effect of resilience and job stress on information security awareness. Inf. Comput. Secur. **26**(3), 277–289 (2018). https://doi.org/10.1108/ICS-03-2018-0032

22. European Court of Auditors, Challenges to effective EU cybersecurity policy (2019). https://www.eca.europa.eu/Lists/ECADocuments/BRP_CYBERSECURITY/BRP_CYBERSECURITY_EN.pdf. Accessed 14 Dec 2021

23. European Economic and Social Committee, 'Cybersecurity: Ensuring awareness and resilience of the private sector across Europe in face of mounting cyber risks'. https://www.eesc.europa.eu/sites/default/files/files/qe-01-18-515-en-n.pdf. Accessed 14 Dec 2021

24. ENISA, Raising awareness of cybersecurity: a key element of national cybersecurity strategies. Publications Office, LU (2021). https://data.europa.eu/doi/10.2824/363629. Accessed May 30 2022

25. Parrish, A., et al.: Global perspectives on cybersecurity education for 2030: a case for a meta-discipline. In: Proceedings Companion of the 23rd Annual ACM Conference on Innovation and Technology in Computer Science Education, New York, NY, USA, Jul. 2018, pp. 36–54 (2018). https://doi.org/10.1145/3293881.3295778

A Competency Definition Based on the Knowledge, Skills, and Human Dispositions Constructs

Teresa Pereira[1]([⊠]) [ID], António Amaral[2] [ID], and Isabel Mendes[1]

[1] Centro ALGORITMI, Universidade do Minho, Guimarães, Portugal
tpereira@dsi.uminho.pt, mimp@ua.pt

[2] INESC TEC—Institute for Systems and Computer Engineering, Technology and Science,
4200-465 Porto, Portugal
antonio.m.amaral@inesctec.pt

Abstract. The competency-based learning approach arose from the Bologna signed declaration. However, a competency definition has never been easy and has been evolving and adapted over time, from indicators and learning goals to learning outcomes, which were formulated in terms of competencies. Meanwhile, the competency concept becomes discussed by pears, in particular, associating knowledge, skills, and human dispositions or attitudes into the competency definition. This information will be an essential update to the previous approaches and certainly contribute to achieving more accurate and reliable competencies information for employers and higher education institutions (HEI). This paper aims to reinforce the relevance of these concepts and suggest how each construct of "knowledge, skills and human dispositions" could be approached to formulate a competency. In addition, due to accelerated digital transformation, an example of a digital competency defined by the DigComp 2.0 framework, with proposed information regarding each of the three constructs, will be presented to consolidate this challenge. As future work, it is intended to analyze the eight different levels, and competency profiles defined by the European Qualification Framework (EQF) and assign a profile to each defined competency. In the end, it is expected altogether to contribute to achieving a competency roadmap definition.

Keywords: Competency · Knowledge · Skill · Human disposition or attitudes · Knowledge-based learning · Project-based learning · Competency-based learning · Computing curricula 2020 · Micro-credentials · *DigComp*

1 Introduction

More than 20 years ago, the Bologna Declaration was signed, which created a profound level of reforms to HEI, which besides other aspects, advocates a competency-based learning approach aiming to promote the overall development of students, both in specific and transversal competencies. The summarized vision guidelines rely on redesigning curricular programs and methods to promote learning to know, learning to do, learning to live

T. Pereira et al. (Eds.): IoECon 2022, LNICST 458, pp. 29–38, 2023.
https://doi.org/10.1007/978-3-031-25222-8_3

together, and learning to be, towards enabling students to adapt and successfully address the issues and changes emerging in a complex globalized world [1]. The European Union (EU) national bodies, education authorities, and quality assurance agencies have developed regulations and new program outcomes for accreditation of educational systems based on academic quality standards, such as Framework for Qualifications of the European Higher Education Area [2] as well as the European Qualification Framework for Life-long-learning [3] which are structured in terms of competencies and learning outcomes that graduates should obtain, of an accredited course, as the educational base for practicing their profession. HEI redesigned its curriculums for qualifications approval and accreditation reviews through the definition of several learning goals formulated and aligned with teaching and assessment methodologies. Two decades after this process began, the research community returned to this topic. It restarted the discussion of the competency-based learning concept expanding competency to the constructs of knowledge, skills, and human disposition or attitudes.

The relevance of the last construct, "human disposition or attitudes", is highlighted due to its impact on knowledge and skills performance. The universal acceptance of global diversity and cultural sensitivity, which are essential in all domains, turn the human dispositions or attitudes in conjunction with knowledge and skills the major challenge to comprise a competency definition. This is what employers have been *"crying to the moon"* for several years. This paper aims to highlight the importance of these concepts for the competencies design based on the competency model proposed by the ACM/IEEE Computing Curricula 2020 [13] and thus address the fundamentals of the Bologna restructuring. Furthermore, an approach is proposed to formulate a competency-based competency based on the three constructs: knowledge, skills, and human dispositions. To achieve this goal and due to the novelty of this theme, a literature review was carried out to increase the quality and promote long learning education through the micro-credentials project [4].

The paper is structured as follows: Sect. 2 will be presented an overview of the learning transition to competency-based learning; Sect. 3 presents a proposed example of knowledge, skills, and human dispositions to comprise a digital competency defined by the *DigComp2.0* framework; conclusions and future work are presented in Sect. 4.

2 Overview on Education Paradigm in HEI (Higher Education Institutions)

The COVID-19 context accelerated the technological necessity, challenging new career opportunities and demanding far more from the HEI's capability to adjust or formulate curricula guidelines to quickly respond to those needs. The face-to-face courses and the large number of online educational courses offered worldwide by HEI have contributed to increasing the number of graduates and responding with knowledge workers highly required by the industry and raised by the emergence of Industry 4.0. The MICROBOL project (Micro-credentials linked to the Bologna key commitments) is related to the aims of the new Erasmus + Programme and the European Higher Education Area (EHEA) to promote continuous learning for all learners, regardless of age or experience. The EHEA intends to increase the recognized quality and quantity of micro-credentials offered by different educational organizations and employers to promote and facilitate continuous learning and competencies acquisition [4]. The primary strategy is to introduce a new mindset, meaning that when a student graduates, he/she gets the degree and starts working but must continuously get micro-credentials to certify new competencies and change the idea that when a degree is achieved, no additional studies are considered necessary to develop their work, job or task.

This approach is strictly related to the individual characters and qualities of each employee. The individual behaviour, attitudes, values, motivation, and self-reflection expected in the workplace or academic activities are the most challenging and complex to teach but assumed by society and expected of every graduate. These individual qualities are the employer's first requirement, followed by technical knowledge. Employers seek employees with unique qualities to be effective in a job, role, function, task, or duty. Actually, the universal acceptance of global diversity and cultural sensitivity, which are essential in all fields, make human dispositions in conjunction with knowledge and skills the significant challenge for attaining a competency definition.

An overview of the learning transition to competency-based learning emphasizing an individual's intellectual, social, or moral tendencies in association with knowledge and skills introduced in the following sub-sections.

2.1 Learning Transition: From Passive to Active Approaches

Historically, the learning process and the knowledge management within HEI have been somehow static, with extremely low-tech inclusion and focused on passive approaches. Professors who were seen as stand-alone actors had been having a capital role in this learning ecosystem, especially by assuming the learning diffusion within the students' community.

In fact, the classical model of student learning fostered a knowledge transfer process in which it is mostly explicit and passively embedded. This factor restricts the learning potential and does not ensure the integral development of individuals' learning process, as it is often excessively theoretical and abstract. Therefore, given the significant variability of learning contexts and different existing combinations of restrictions, the passive approaches demonstrated a low level of effectiveness and, more importantly, showed that they were deeply misaligned with real-world companies' needs and expectations, and requirements.

Notwithstanding, the number of different stakeholders involved in the learning context was commonly scarce or deliberately omitted due to the assumption of not being relevant or needed. This contributed to increasing the gap between the real-world competencies' development and the knowledge gained within the HEI were getting broader, and huger.

A side effect emerged from this asymmetry, and the relationships and realities' perceptions between HEIs and businesses were fragile. An important consequence of this hiatus was the lack of competencies available in the market, which somehow limited the innovation potential and the value creation by the business teams. An excellent example of something that is helping to reduce this difficulty is the University-Industry Collaboration [5], wherein members of academia and industry professionals work collaboratively on a specific problem or challenge and are organized in research and innovation projects.

Therefore, towards potentiating the competency creation, the main scope of the pedagogical agenda of HEI could be the knowledge capture and gaining skills result of the learning achieved. The following topic will address the importance of having proper learning and knowledge creation ecosystem/environment with the involvement of all stakeholders that could positively affect knowledge creation.

2.2 Problem/Project-Based Learning

The transition between the knowledge-based learning paradigm and the appearance of new approaches that could enhance the knowledge and skills creation, especially by applying a context whether the learning environment guarantees active participation of the members involved and details a more specific condition in which they could have the contextual stimulus towards applying their knowledge and evolving their skills [6].

The problem-based learning emerged with enhanced visibility in the last quarter of the XX century by being applied in specific learning contexts for training health professionals [7]. The context-specific problems were extremely helpful in leading to an enduring understanding of the knowledge and skills students will need in a real-world scenario outside the classroom [8]. Despite its relevance, problem-based learning mainly focuses on scenario assessment within a single subject (limited scope) and a shorter time spent on obtaining a valid solution.

Otherwise, in project-based learning, the project team members are deeply involved in the learning process and attain their goals through social interactions and by sharing their knowledge and understanding in a multidiscipline nature [7]. Thus, the context of learning is provided within real-world practices [9], with the expected level of uncertainty and complexity in which human dispositions or attitudes could have a major role in skills development.

The ability to introduce the right type and amount of technology into the learning environment will be essential to attaining 21st-century workforce competencies. The technology domain is vast and could be applied to support meaningful learning namely it could be a key player in the learning process. In this way, the project members can learn by using technology in its multiple possibilities, present or future, not just learning from it [10].

2.3 Competency-Based Learning

The competency definition has recently become of much interest to the research community and discussed the semantic meaning to formulate a competency. The concept of competency has overlapped with the skilled term. In practice, these two concepts are generally assumed with the same meaning and are very difficult to distinguish. The Cambridge dictionary defines competence as "the ability to do something well". In contrast, a skill is defined as "the ability to do an activity or job well, especially because you have done it many times" [11]. The skills are proficiencies developed through training and experiences. They are associated with practice (hours or days of practice) to master a skill, whereas competency is a much broader concept than skills. Competencies involve skills, knowledge and human abilities that, combined with behaviours demonstrate the ability to perform a task effectively and successfully. A summary comparison between competencies and skills is presented in Table 1.

Table 1. Competencies versus skills, adapted from [12].

Competencies	Skills
Competencies are a combination of skills, knowledge, and human abilities or dispositions that make an individual successful in a job	Skills are learned or acquired through training knowledge is needed towards completing a specific task
Indicate how a task is performed effectively and successfully	Indicate what talents or abilities an individual needs to complete a specific task

The Computing Curricula 2020 report published, on December 31 of 2020, by ACM and IEEE Computing Society, introduces the competency-based learning approach with three constructs – knowledge, skill, and human disposition- to be included in a competency definition [13]. Accordingly, to the authors of this report, a competency definition should comprise three things an individual must possess to be effective in a job, role, function, or duty within a given context or task, represented as follows:

Competency = Knowledge + Skills + Dispositions.

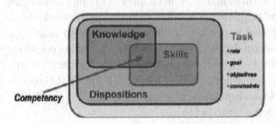

Fig. 1. Conceptual structure of the computing curricula 2020 competency model, source [13]

Knowledge. In a competency definition, the enumerated knowledge should answer the question "know-what", meaning "what is the subject matter a student must know to do a task or perform a role?". In practice, knowledge comprises proficiency in core concepts and content and the application of learning to new and unexpected situations. This construct refers to the list of topics teachers define in the syllabi according to the courses created by departments to offer in their academic program the accreditation agencies, which stipulate the accreditation criteria and employers identify in job descriptions [13].

Skills. A skill expresses a practical dimension of knowledge to define the "know-how" construct. This means identifying the capacities that should be exploited towards enabling students to know how to apply knowledge to accomplish a task actively. This construct is related to the ability to carry out tasks with determined results, requiring time and practice to develop them. The acquisition of "know-what" trained or experienced by "know-how" combines knowledge and skills constructs [13].

Human Dispositions. Human dispositions are related to the question of "know-why". It is related to intellectual (e.g., School of thought such as Engineering, Social Science, Medical Sciences, et cetera), social (e.g., differences in how people have been brought up/raised, behavioural culture, and social dynamics), and moral or ethical tendencies. The human disposition will be influenced by how people have been raised, e.g., family values, the cultural and social dynamics an individual has been exposed to the ethical and moral standards associated with the character in task performance. The human temperament balances or influences the behaviour of applying "know-what" (knowledge) that becomes "know-how" (skill) [13].

The EQF also introduces these concepts separately. While knowledge is described as theoretical and factual, skills are described as being cognitive and practical. A cognitive skill refers to logical, intuitive, and creative thinking, while practical involves manual agility combined with the help of methods, materials, tools, and instruments. In addition, to knowledge and skill, EQF associates responsibility and autonomy as required elements to enable the learner to apply knowledge [14]. Individual qualities, responsibility, and autonomy are highly relevant and are always needed for any job application. However, there are other equality relevant such as the capacity to adapt, collaboration meaning the ability and motivation to work with others, look beyond simple solutions, a strong commitment to goal-driven, achieve goals, self-motivated, determination, et cetera. Human dispositions are an intrinsic and relevant element in a competency definition. It expresses the institutional and programmatic values expected in the workplace.

The following section presents a practical example to supply evidence of knowledge, skills, and human disposition' proposal to address a competency definition. The competency described is "Protecting personal data and privacy", defined in the European Digital Competencies Framework (DigComp) [15]. The DigComp was selected because since 2013 it has been a European reference for the development and strategic planning of digital competence initiatives [16].

3 Knowledge, Skills, and Human Dispositions to Address the DigComp Competency "Privacy and Personal Data Protection" Defined

The European Commission's Digital Competence Framework 2.0 (DigComp 2.0) identified the key components of digital competence in the five following domains: 1) information and data literacy, 2) communication and collaboration, 3) digital content creation, 4) safety, and 5) problem solving [15]. Furthermore, within each domain, a set of competencies was defined. For each level of competency definition, the DigComp framework 2.0 introduces one single descriptor to describe knowledge, skill, and attitudes jointly. In the scope of the DigComp, the third construct is labelled as "attitudes", while in this paper, it is referred to as "human disposition", which follows the approach defined in the CC2020 report. This paper's major challenge and novelty are clearly on defining knowledge, skills, and human dispositions within one competency definition.

To evidence this challenge, the competency :"4.2 Protecting personal data and privacy" was selected, and defined by the DigComp 2.0 framework, as the second digital competency of 4 competencies defined within competence area 4 "Safety".

The DigComp 2.0 framework summarises the "Safety" area as: "*To protect devices, content, personal data, and privacy in digital environments. To protect physical and psychological health, and to be aware of digital technologies for social well-being and social inclusion. To be aware of the environmental impact of digital technologies and their use.*" [8]. To comprise this description, DigComp splits the "Safety" area into four competencies, namely: 1) protecting devices; 2) protecting personal data and privacy; 3) protecting health and well-being, and 4) protecting the environment.

Focusing on competency 2: "protecting personal data and privacy" DigComp2.0 defines this competency with the following descriptor: "*To protect personal data and privacy in digital environments. To understand how to use and share personally identifiable information while being able to protect oneself and others from damage. To understand that digital services use a "Privacy policy" to inform how personal data is used.*" [15].

Analysing this defined competency and identifying or extracting from this description the knowledge, skills, and human dispositions is extremely difficult, which may suggest or raise questions and different interpretations. In practice, this competency' description is the same approach followed since the establishment of the Bologna Process, the difference is in the names, e.g., learning outcomes, goals, indicators, et cetera. Although, it is important to highlight that the DigComp framework regards the definition of digital competencies, which has greater importance in the current digital context. In this paper, the authors intend to trigger the awareness of the fact a competency definition must or should embrace the intersection of knowledge, skills, and human dispositions.

In this context, and towards embracing this challenge, a proposal for the three constructs will be formulated to the defined competency of "protecting personal data and privacy".

Starting with knowledge description and addressing the question *Know-What*, the knowledge for "protecting personal data and privacy" competency is on:

- Knowing the information security properties (confidentiality, integrity, and availability) and others' properties like authentication, accountability, and no repudiation.
- Knowing the access mechanisms for authentication (passwords, biometrics, et cetera) and their requirements;
- Knowing and applying information security policies and requirements;
- Knowing the standards and good practices of safety and regulations.

  Accordingly, to the knowledge previously described, the enumerated skills were defined to respond to the question "*Know-how*", which are as follows proposed:
- Apply the adequate security policies to protect the information security properties, confidentiality, integrity, and availability, as well as to protect personal and sensitive information;
- Apply security policies that ensure data privacy to comply with regulations, for example, the General Data Protection Regulation (GDPR);
- Apply security good practices and standard guidelines.

Lastly, the human dispositions identified as relevant may influence and contribute to the successful achievement and integration of previously defined knowledge and skills. Following the previous approaches, the human dispositions were defined to address or respond to the question "know-why":

- Adjustable – the capability to adjust in response to change;
- Collaborative – the capability to work with others;
- Strong commitment;
- Communicative;
- Ethical.

The human dispositions definition is a major challenge. It is undoubtedly the relevance and the impact of human dispositions on knowledge and skills acquisition. Dispositions are an intrinsic component of competency; it represents an opportunity to express institutional and programmatic values expected in the workplace. The association of the human dispositions' description to a competency reveals a clear commitment to self-reflection and examination that distinguishes a competency from a learning outcome.

Figure 2 illustrates the described competency definition, highlighting the intersection of the three constructs and the dispositions component embracing the knowledge and skills constructs.

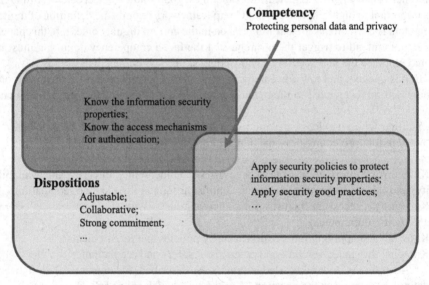

Fig. 2. Competency definition, adapted from [13].

4   Conclusions and Future Work

The rapid evolvement of technological applications with the decreased financial costs of technological gadgets promotes speed and accessibility to information and new

Internet-enabled services, accelerated by the digital transformation challenge of the learning process. Despite being pointed out in the past through the Bologna Declaration, competency-based learning is still not consensual and broadly understood by multiple stakeholders involved in competency development. Bloom's Taxonomy identifies characteristics aligned with "know-how" and "know-why", where each level (i.e.: remember, understand, apply, analyze, evaluate, and create) articulates an attitude toward engaging knowledge [17]. This reveals that still is a lot to be done to identify the potential paths that promote the adequate development of competencies, both for the sphere of the individual or the group.

Simultaneously, the digital transformation process will ensure that it is possible to develop new teaching and learning approaches that could be more personalized and aligned toward enhancing the individual's knowledge [18] whether these could be by using digital twins, supported by virtual and augmented reality that can accelerate the process of converting information into knowledge. Throughout time the technology will allow the usage and analysis of the longitudinal data from the interaction with digital equipment and with an intelligence layer to help identify the appropriate context for developing and enhancing knowledge into skills. Furthermore, identifying the attitudes and behavioural characteristics that, at the individual level, will allow better efficiency and performance and, in this way, support the transition from skills to competencies.

In future work, it would be relevant to study in detail the multi-layers of the digital transformation competencies, the right way to measure them and propose a roadmap for its adoption. A technological environment should be created to support an individual and group diagnosis to potentiate the individual performance.

Acknowledgement. This work has been supported by FCT – *Fundação para a Ciência e Tecnologia* within the R&D Units Project Scope: UIDB/00319/2020.

References

1. Delors, J.: Learning: the treasure within; report to UNESCO of International Commission on Education for the Twenty-first Century (highlights). UNESCO Publishing (1996). https://une sdoc.unesco.org/ark:/48223/pf0000109590. Accessed 20 Oct 2021
2. Bologna Working Group on Qualifications Frameworks, *A Framework for Qualifications of the European Higher Education Area* (Copenhagen: Ministry of Science, Technology and Innovation, 2005). http://ecahe.eu/w/images/7/76/A_Framework_for_Qualifica tions_for_the_European_Higher_Education_Area.pdf
3. E Commission The European Qualifications Framework for Lifelong Learning (EQF) Publications Office of the European Union Luxembourg (2008)
4. MICROBOL Recommendations On Micro-Credentials. https://microcredentials.eu/. Accessed 07 Dec 2020
5. Fernandes, G., Amaral, A., Peixoto, J., Pinto, E.B., Araújo, M., Machado, R.J.: Key initiatives to successfully manage collaborative university-industry R&D: IC-HMI case study. Procedia Comput. Sci. **164**, 414–423 (2019). https://doi.org/10.1016/j.procs.2019.12.201
6. Hallinger, P.: Mapping continuity and change in the intellectual structure of the knowledge base on problem-based learning, 1974–2019: A systematic review. Br. Educ. Res. J. **46**(6), 1423–1444 (2020). https://doi.org/10.1002/berj.3656

7. Kokotsaki, D., Menzies, V., Wiggins, A.: Project-based learning: a review of the literature. Improving Schools **19**(3), 267–277 (2016). https://doi.org/10.1177/1365480216659733

8. Hung, W.: All PBL starts here: the problem. Interdisc. J. Prob. Based Learn. 10(2), 2 (2016). https://doi.org/10.7771/1541-5015.1604

9. Al-Balushi, S.M., Al-Aamri, S.S.: The effect of environmental science projects on students' environmental knowledge and science attitudes. Int. Res. Geog. Environ. Educ. **23**(3), 213–227 (2014)

10. Rahmawati, A., Suryani, N., Akhyar, M., Sukarmin.: Technology-integrated project-based learning for pre-service teacher education: a systematic literature review. Open Eng. **10**(1), 620–629 (2020). https://doi.org/10.1515/eng-2020-0069

11. Cambridge Dictionary. https://dictionary.cambridge.org/dictionary/english/. Accessed 20 Dec 2021

12. Hasa. PEDIAA. What is the difference between competencies and skills (2021). https://pediaa.com/what-is-the-difference-between-competencies-and-skills/. Accessed 27 Dec 2021

13. Clear, A., Parrish, A., Impagliazzo, J., Wang, P.: Computing Curricula 2020: Paradigms for Global Computing Education, 1st edn. Association for Computing Machinery, New York (2020)

14. Europass European Union – Description on the eight EQF levels. https://europa.eu/europass/en/description-eight-eqf-levels. Accessed 12 Aug 2021

15. EU Science HUB. The European Commission's science and knowledge service. The Digital Competence Framework 2.0 (2019). https://ec.europa.eu/jrc/en/digcomp/digital-competence-framework. Accessed 18 Mar 2021

16. Carretero, S., Vuorikari, R., Punie, Y.: DigComp 2.1: The digital competence framework for citizens with eight proficiency levels and examples of use. JCR Science Hub, JCR106281. (2017). ISSN 1831–9424. https://doi.org/10.2760/38842. Luxembourg: Publication Office of the European Union

17. © European Union, 2017

18. Waguespack, L., Topi, H., Frezza, S.: Adopting competency mindful of professionalism in baccalaureate computing curricula. In: Proceedings of the EDSIG Conference. Cleveland Ohio (2019). ISSN 2473, pp. 3857 v5 n4955

19. Santos, H., Pereira, T., Mendes, I.: Challenges and reflections in designing cyber security curriculum. IEEE World Eng. Educ. Conf. (EDUNINE) **2017**, 47–51 (2017). https://doi.org/10.1109/EDUNINE.2017.7918179

The Influence of the Image and Photography of E- Commerce Products on the Purchase Decision of Online Consumers

Manuel Sousa Pereira[1]([✉]) [iD], António Cardoso[2] [iD], Carlota Fernandes[1],
Sandra Rodrigues[1], and Frederico D'Orey[3]

[1] Polytechnic Institute of Viana do Castelo, Viana do Castelo, Portugal
msousa.manuel@gmail.com
[2] University Fernando Pessoa, Porto, Portugal
[3] University Portucalense, Porto, Portugal

Abstract. This work had as main objective to understand the importance of photography for online sales, as well as to verify the power of the image in the decision of a purchase, regarding the attraction and loyalty of customers, especially through social networks and online sales platforms, which are today one of the main tools for sales from e-commerce. Regarding methodology, a questionnaire was conducted, consisting of 32 questions, through Google Forms, in order to collect the opinion about the influence of photography in e-commerce. An initial pre-test was made and, once approved, it was shared in November and December 2021, through a convenience sample, using the following social networks: WhatsApp, Facebook and Instagram. A 217 response was obtained, with the data allowing the conclusion that photography plays an important role when consumers seek to buy over the internet; that image is important in the online purchase decision; that photography in e-commerce acts as an important tool in attracting and retaining customers. The experience of e-commerce even after the pandemic increases more and more, in view of the immersion of society in the virtual world. Photography is a powerful tool for transmitting emotions, also adding emotional factors to advertisements, and through this, conquering intangible values to the product or service.

Keywords: Photography · Image · e-Commerce · Social networks · Consumer behaviour

1 Introduction

E-commerce, mainly through the use of social networks, is a very efficient strategy when it comes to communication and promotion of products (Thaichon et al. 2021; Wagner et al. 2021) mostly free of charge, allowing a quick and easy access to a population that regularly uses these networks (Upadhyay et al. 2022), viewing hundreds of products daily. As a result of this observation, many businessmen and entrepreneurs have begun to

© ICST Institute for Computer Sciences, Social Informatics and Telecommunications Engineering 2023
Published by Springer Nature Switzerland AG 2023. All Rights Reserved
T. Pereira et al. (Eds.): IoECon 2022, LNICST 458, pp. 39–51, 2023.
https://doi.org/10.1007/978-3-031-25222-8_4

invest more in social networks and online platforms for the dissemination and promotion of their products and services.

In this sense, this article aims to identify the importance of image and photography in e-commerce and its influence on the purchase decision. On the other hand, and in specific terms, it seeks to evaluate the importance of the quality of the photograph to make the purchase; the importance of editing, props and quantity of photographs in the sale of the product or service; the importance of reality transmitted through photography; the importance of evaluation in the sales process.

We begin by reviewing the literature on online consumer behavior and the importance of social networks in e-commerce, as well as the use of technical and editing devices to create images and photos that provide a favorable and conducive environment for online shopping. After that, the framework and the methodological process of the research are presented, namely the questionnaire design and its availability through google forms, followed by the analysis and discussion of the results.

2 Theoretical Background

Online consumer behavior is characterized by the mental and emotional activities performed in the selection, purchase, and use of products or services for the satisfaction of needs and wants. There are several internal and external factors that influence consumer buying behavior among them are cultural factors, social factors, personal factors and psychological factors (Soloman, 2019).

The human being in the condition of customer, acts driven more by emotion, more than by reason at the time of consuming, acquiring, some product. In this sense, people are mostly seduced by what they see, through their interpretation and use of images they undergo constant changes, and in this way, the transmission of symbolic images to consumption is characteristic of contemporary culture, where everything is commodified. The meanings change and the artistic vision of the photographer adapts to reality.

The customer in online shopping does not consider important the presence of entertainment elements, in his experience, through the website (Ertemel et al. 2021). Confidentiality and reliability, on the other hand, are of great importance, since the online consumer is particularly concerned about sharing personal data (Zaid and Patwayati, 2021). Information prior to the purchase, about the correct procedure to make it, or if it was really well done are, as well as security, factors valued by the online consumer (Upadhyay et al. 2022).

According to Cardoso and Sissi (2021) customers have the facility to find products without leaving home, then it is necessary to remember that the competition also has this facility, and that the customer will choose the product that is better presented. In this sense, professional photography assumes a prominent role. Thus, it is essential to develop strategies for attracting and winning over customers, seeking their attention and trust. In this sense, all brands that want to enter the online market must have a different strategy and respect the main influences of the online market such as trends, legislation and consumer confidence.

2.1 Photography and Ecommerce

The inclusion of filming and photographing devices in mobile equipment simultaneously with the spread of the internet have contributed to an increasingly present proximity in the relationship between photography and online commerce. According to Rejan and Neves (2018), based on the works of Hoffman and Oliveira (2015), modernity implied modifications in the action of photographing. The diffusion of photography in popular media reached its apex after the advent of the internet and, with the creation of digital culture, there was the inclusion of the camera to mobile devices, which brought great influence on the change of the photographic process.

In a complementary way, the use of photography continues to be a factor of impact and differentiation in the relationship between the consumer and the market, because, as mentioned (Montenegro, 2021), companies use information technology to interconnect and exchange information and data, reducing costs, improving productivity and increasing customer loyalty.

Regarding the relationship between customers and technology, Mariano et al. (2015) refer that with the development of technology and the internet, the use of the digital space to carry out market transactions is getting bigger and more frequent, connecting buyers directly with companies and totally changing the way companies relate to customers and vice versa, creating new values and relationships. With the purpose of placing products and services in the fastest and most interactive way to a larger number of customers, in the various locations of the world, websites are seen as a crucial point of competition among competitors. It is through the website, that the brand conveys and applies its communication and advertising objectives. The website is the core of e-commerce, that is, where it will have to focus its efforts to retain consumers (products (Thaichon et al. 2021; Wagner et al. 2021). According to Pontes, (2018), e-commerce, emerges with the advances in technology that drive changes at various levels, creating new paradigms of purchase. With the popularity of the internet, more and more companies and individuals have joined e-commerce, which is reflected in the high number of sellers and buyers interacting for transactions on the website.

Photography has the power to relive moments, to bring old emotions to the surface, thus making it one of the best forms of visual communication. Photography does not only imply reflecting on a certain type of image or on a system of symbolic exchanges, such reflection requires a better analysis because photography has always proved to be an agent for shaping reality, in a process of assembly and selection, in which the world reveals itself to be "similar" and "different" at the same time. The new language of photography has brought about a real revolution in the digital world and has become a strong business tool, a different aspect in the past, where photography had the objective of showing products, while nowadays it seeks to influence people.

Photography is not only an image, but an image-act, and this "act" is not only limited to the gesture of the production of the image itself, but also includes the act of its reception and contemplation, in short as inseparable from its whole enunciation, as an image experience, as a totally programmatic goal (Rejan and Neves, 2018).

2.2 Social Networks and e-commerce

Regarding the use of photography on social media, we can see that Instagram is a very important sharing platform that engages consumers (Almeida, 2021). According to Pereira (2014). "It is an application that allows users to take photos, apply filters and effects, and share them on a variety of social networks, such as Twitter and Facebook. The Instagram application was born with the purpose of encouraging the production and editing of digital photographs through mobile phones (Melo, 2019), allowing a new dynamic in the relationship of the individual with the image, in the sharing and dissemination of photographic content through virtual means (Lima, 2014).

Regarding the use of Instagram in the relationship with the consumer, we can verify that the buying experience begins, most of the time, in the search made in social networks, through impactful images and with visual impact (Melo, 2019). Fashion represents for the individual, its visual character, with valuable images and good appearances, tools with the visual features such as those of Instagram allow "ordinary" people to approach the public, create trust and empathy with the real stories of their daily lives and gain many followers (Pinto, 2018).

3 Methodology

To carry out this work, a literature review was conducted on this object of study, through the exploration of the thematic collection available scientific databases, seeking to systematize a set of ideals, studies and relevant considerations about this area of knowledge and that allowed to define the conceptual and methodological framework of the research (Malhotra, 2019).

As previously mentioned, the overall objective of this research is to understand the importance of photography in online sales (e-commerce), and in particular, verify the power of the image in the decision of a purchase, regarding the attraction and loyalty of customers, mainly through social networks and online sales platforms.

Thus, the following research questions were defined: (1) Do image and photography influence the purchase decision? (2) Does the quality of photography facilitate brand memorization? (3) Do props and textual information support online sales? (4) Does the amount of photography help create a favorable image and confidence in the product? (5) Does excessive editing take away veracity and diminish credibility to the product? (6) Does the congruence between the advertised image and the actual product (verified upon receipt of the product) promote loyalty and repeat purchase?

In order to answer the objectives and research questions, we developed an exploratory study with descriptive design (Pestana and Gageiro, 2014; Malhotra, 2019), using the questionnaire as an instrument to collect information. The questionnaire, composed of 32 questions, was developed through Google forms, and was structured in four blocks: 4 questions on socio-demographic data (gender, age, marital status, education), 11 questions on the importance of image and photography (using a 5-point Likert scale, where 1 was strongly disagree and 5 strongly agree), 4 questions on technical issues (yes/no dichotomous scale), and 4 multiple choice.

A pre-test was conducted with 12 consumers, seeking to eliminate typos, and reorganize the structure of the questionnaire (Pestana and Gageiro, 2014; Malhotra, 2019), improving the questions presented and the most relevant considerations for the understanding of this theme.

After being approved it was shared, in the months of November and December 2021, through a convenience sample (Malhotra, 2019) using the following social networks, WhatsApp, Facebook and Instagram. We obtained 217 valid responses, which is considered an acceptable number that allows the analysis and statistical treatment of the data.

4 Results

As can be seen in the Table 1, the respondents were mostly female (84.3%), with 34 male respondents (15.7%). In terms of age, it can be seen that the "26–35 years old" age group had 74 respondents (34.1%), followed by the "18–25 years old" age group (29.5%), then the "36–45 years old" age group (22.1%), and there were few respondents below the age of 18 (1.8%) and above the age of 55 (2.3%).

The vast majority of respondents are single (65.9%), with 66 married (30.4%) and eight divorced (3.7%). Regarding academic qualifications, it appears that most respondents have a high school degree (54.8%). This is followed by respondents with a Bachelor's degree (20.7%) and a 3rd cycle degree (10.1%).

Table 1. Sample

		F	%
Gender	Male	34	15,7
	Female	183	84,3
Age groups	< 18 years	4	1,8
	18–25 years	64	29,5
	26–35 years	74	34,1
	36–45 years	48	22,1
	46–55 years	22	10,1
	> 55 years	5	2,3
Marital status	Single	143	65,9
	Married	66	30,4
	Divorced	8	3,7
Qualification	2nd cycle	2	,9
	3rd cycle	22	10,1

(continued)

Table 1. (*continued*)

	F	%
Secondary education	119	54,8
Bachalaureate	10	4,6
Graduation	45	20,7
Masters	19	8,8

The scale shows good internal consistency, having obtained a Cronbach's alpha of 803.

Overall the respondents agreed with the prepositions presented, with percentages of total agreement higher than 44% (Table 2). If we take into account that the values of disagreement are very low, it is possible to conclude that respondents recognize the value and importance of image and photography in the commercial initiatives of online companies.

Table 2. Frequencies

Items	Strongly disagree 1	Disagree 2	Undecided 3	Agree 4	Strongly agree 5	M	SD
	F (%)	F (%)	F (%)	F (%)	F (%)		
A quality image conveys credibility		2 (0.9)	21 (9,7)	45 (20,7)	149 (68,7)	4,58	,698
The quality of the photograph has power in the purchase decision		1 (0,5)	11 (5,1)	49 (22,6)	156 (71,9)	4,66	,597
A salesperson who presents a quality photograph is more likely to be remembered by the customer	1 (0,5)		6 (2,8)	51 (23,5)	159 (73,3)	**4,69**	,570

(*continued*)

Table 2. (*continued*)

Items	Strongly disagree 1	Disagree 2	Undecided 3	Agree 4	Strongly agree 5	M	SD
	F (%)	F (%)	F (%)	F (%)	F (%)		
When the product reaches the consumer and is the same as in the photograph, this leads the consumer to repeat the experience again			5 (2,3)	21 (9,7)	191 (88)	**4,86**	,408
The color of the photograph influences the purchase	1 (0,5)	3 (1,4)	19 (8,8)	64 (29,5)	130 (59,9)	4,47	,753
Lighting influences the quality of the photograph and consequently the purchase of the article	1 (0,5)		10 (4,6)	62 (28,6)	144 (66,4)	4,61	,600
It is important to follow a photographic composition	1 (0,5)		29 (13,4)	72 (33,2)	115 (53)	4,39	,732
Image focus is important in photography			7 (3,2)	47 (21,7)	163 (75,1)	**4,72**	,518
Textual information is important when purchasing the article	1 (0,5)		16 (7,4)	55 (25,3)	144 (66,4)	4,58	,649
The use of props supports the sale of the product	2 (0,9)	6 (2,8)	41 (18,9)	72 (33,2)	96 (44,2)	4,18	,893

(*continued*)

Table 2. (*continued*)

Items	Strongly disagree 1	Disagree 2	Undecided 3	Agree 4	Strongly agree 5	M	SD
	F (%)	F (%)	F (%)	F (%)	F (%)		
The number of product photographs is important	2 (0,9)	5 (2,3)	38 (17,5)	65 (30)	107 (49,3)	4,25	,885

Thus, respondents agree that a quality image conveys credibility (M^1 = 4.58; SD^2:0.698), the quality of the photograph influences the purchase decision (M = 4.66; SD = 0.597) and memorization (M = 4.69; SD = 0.570) and upon receipt of the product, checking the correspondence with the advertised image promotes repeat purchase (M = 4.86; SD = 0.408).

Similarly, respondents agree that color of the photograph influences the act of purchase (M = 4.47, SD = 0.753), lighting has an influence on the quality of the photograph and, consequently, on the purchase of the product (M = 4.61; SD = 0.6), being important to follow a photographic composition (M = 4.39; SD = 0.732) where, in complementary terms, the textual information (M = 4.58; SD = 0.649)) and the use of props (M = 4.18; SD = 0.893) support the sale of the product.

It should also be noted that respondents consider that the focus of the image (M = 4.72; SD = 0.518) and the amount of product photos (M = 4.25; SD = 0.885) are important in selling products online.

As shown in the following Table 3, respondents recognize the importance of technology and image professionals that allow the consumer to make a good evaluation of the product and support it in the purchase decision, and photography is fundamental in the purchase decision (76.5%).

Thus, 208 respondents (95.6%) consider important to invest in image professionals (photography) who use appropriate technology (tripod, light sources) to maintain a quality to the reality of the product (74.2%), because the use of flash influences the quality of photography (85.7%) and the use of image editors (57.6%) is important in the purchase decision.

However, respondents consider that excessive editing takes away from the veracity of the product (76%).

Therefore, the majority of respondents consider that on platforms like AliExpress (online shopping platform) it is important to see the evaluation of products by customers to help the purchase of others (81.1%).

---

[1] M = Mean.

[2] SD = Standard Deviation.

Table 3. Frequencies

Items	Yes 1	No 2	Other 3
	F (%)	F (%)	F (%)
Is it important to invest in a professional?	208 (95,6)	6 (2,8)	3 (1,4)
In order to maintain a quality to the reality of the product will it be necessary to use a tripod, light sources (lamps, soft box…)?	161 (74,2)	50 (23)	6 (2,8)
Does the use of flash influence the quality of the photo?	186 (85,7)	24 (11,1)	7 (3,2)
Is the use of image editors an important factor in the purchase decision?	125 (57,6)	38 (17,5)	15 (6,9)
Is photography fundamental in the buying decision	166 (76,5)	7 (3,2)	11 (5,1)
Does excessive editing take away from the	165 (76)	7 (3,2)	11 (5,1)
On platforms like AliExpress (online shopping platform) is it important to see customer reviews of products to help others buy?	176 (81,1)	2 (0,9)	-.

For 170 respondents (78.3%) it is necessary for the photography to convey the "story" of the brand to captivate the consumer (Table 4) so the scenarios (Table 5) not only help in selling the product but also demonstrate the product in a real environment (53%).

Table 4. Is it necessary for photography to convey the "story" of the brand to captivate the consumer?

Items	F	%
Yes, so that the customer has more confidence in his purchase	170	78,3
No, the history" of the brand has no influence on the purchase	39	17,1

Table 5. Does the use of scenery influence the sale of the product?

Items	F	%
The scenarios not only help in selling the product but also demonstrate the product in a real environment.	115	53,0
The scenario has no influence whatsoever on the moment of purchase.	6	2,8
Depending on the type of product the setting can be an asset or not.	86	39,6
Depending on the emotional state of the buyer the scenario can lead to the creation of a stronger connection with the brand.	10	4,6

To achieve high photo quality, respondents consider that a good camera achieves better results (80.2%), although some (19.8%) say that there are other similar alternatives to achieve good results (Table 6).

Table 6. Do you think the brand of the camera influences the quality of the photo?

Items	F	%
Yes, a good machine can achieve better results	174	80,2
No, there are other similar alternatives to achieve good results	43	19,8

The vast majority of respondents (90.3%) consider that the photo is a key point in closing the sale online and therefore relevant in e-commerce, although for 15 respondents (6.9%) the photo may be a relevant point, but the textual information is more relevant (Table 7).

Table 7. Do you think it is relevant to have photographs in e-commerce?

Items	F	%
Without a doubt, photography is a key point in closing the sale online	196	90,3
There is no relationship between the photograph and the sale of the product	4	1,8
This may be a relevant point, but the textual information has greater relevance	15	6,9

Finally, in the case of seasonal products, 96 respondents (44.3%) consider it important and or very important (M = 4.10; SD = 1.035) that the photo is able to reflect the seasonality of the product (Table 8).

Table 8. Frequencies

Items	Nothing important 1	Little important 2	Neither little nor very important 3	Important 4	Very important 5	M	SD
	F (%)	F (%)	F (%)	F (%)	F (%)		
If the product is seasonal, how important is it for the photography to reflect the seasonality of the product?	6 (2,8)	1 (0,5)	22 (10,1)	42 (19,4)	54 (24,9)	4,10	1,035

Thus, the results of our study reinforce the conclusions already identified in the literature in similar studies, namely regarding the importance of the experience with the website (Ertemel et al. 2021; Upadhyay, et al. 2022), in which the image of the products presented (photography quality) on the website contributes to the formation of the company's brand image and can influence the purchase decision (Cardoso and Sissi, 2021).

Likewise, the integration of technologies (internet and mobile equipment) and media (text, videos and photographs) promotes interaction, involvement and relationship between the company and consumers, as evidenced in the literature (Hoffman and Oliveira, 2015; Rejan and Neves, 2018; Pinto, 2018; Melo, 2019).

This approach allows not only to reduce costs, but is also decisive in identifying and differentiating the brand (and the company), increasing productivity, retention and consumer loyalty (Montenegro, 2021; Thaichon et al. 2021; Wagner et al. 2021).

In line with the study by Rejan and Neves (2018), the data confirm the importance and value of photography in the reception·and contemplation of images, allowing the best way to interpret the narrative and discourse of brands. In fact, photographs manage to create greater involvement and proximity to the consumer, as evidenced by Almeida (2021).

5   Conclusions

The development of this study has enabled an analysis of how photography is an important factor in e-commerce. The need for online sales and the demand for knowledge in e-commerce during the pandemic increased considerably. In view of this analysis of the results, professional photography is something indispensable when making a purchase and 60.3% of the respondents are motivated by photography in the purchase decision.

The respondents recognize the importance of technology and professional image professionals that allow the consumer to make a good evaluation of the product and support him in the purchase decision, and photography is fundamental in the purchase decision (76.5%).

The majority of respondents (95.6%) consider it important to invest in image professionals (photography) that allow them to maintain a quality to the reality of the product (74.2%), because the use of flash influences the quality of the photograph (85.7%) and the use of image editors (57.6%) is important in the buying decision. However, respondents consider that excessive editing takes away from the veracity of the product (76%).

The experience of e-commerce even after the pandemic increases more and more, in view of the immersion of society in the virtual world, most people (81.1%) have become accustomed to online shopping and, therefore, considering the facts and results presented, the investment in professional photography of products and services is essential for the success of sales and customer loyalty, ensuring customer satisfaction through strategic images.

In this sense, photography is a powerful tool for transmitting emotions, also adding emotional factors to advertisements, and through this, conquering intangible values to the product or service.

The results of this study can be of interest to all companies that are making the digital transition, namely regarding the use of photography and image to produce positive experiences for consumers. Likewise, companies that already use this media can improve their online communication strategies, giving greater importance to photography and its importance in transmitting the brand's personality and building the relationship with the customer.

This study had as main limitations the use of a convenience sample, mostly female, lacking a qualitative study for a better understanding of the theme.

Thus, it is recommended that, in future research, a larger sample is used, with a balance between genders, focusing on a specific group of consumers (for example, young people and/or young adults).

On the other hand, future studies should be deepened on the impact of photography in creating an online customer experience.

1. References

Almeida, B.: Power of a lifestyle micro-influencer in changing followers' behavior on Instagram and Youtube. Master's dissertation from Instituto Superior de Contabilidade e Administração do Porto (2021). http://hdl.handle.net/10400.22/19553

Cardoso, M., Sissi, S.: The impact of photography on digital marketing. Facit Bus. Technol. J. Edn. 31, 1, 333–350 (2021). http://revistas.faculdadefacit.edu.br/index.php/JNT

Ertemel, A.V., Civelek, M.E., Pektaş, E., G.O.¨, C.emberci M,: The role of customer experience in the effect of online flow state on customer loyalty. PLoS ONE 16(7), e0254685 (2021). https://doi.org/10.1371/journal.pone.0254685

Hoffmann, M.L., Oliveira, M.: Photography in the age of technical incompetence. Rev Famecos (Online). Porto Alegre. 22(4) (2015). https://doi.org/10.15448/1980-3729.2015.4.20524

Lima, H. (2014). The contributions of Instagram in shaping the digital culture of contemporary society. Master's dissertation, Methodist University of Piracicaba

Malhotra, N.: Marketing Research: An Applied Orientation, 7th edn. Pearson, New York (2019)

Mariano, A., Paiva, C., Souza, R., Silva, L.: Online word-of-mouth marketing (eWOM): concepts, background and delimitations. In: Conference: International Congress of Administration At: Paraná (2015). https://doi.org/10.13140/RG.2.1.2280.6487

Melo, J.: Women's fashion: a study on the impact of Instagram on the purchase decision process. Master in Communication Sciences, branch of Public Relations, Advertising and Marketing (2019). http://hdl.handle.net/10284/7804

Montenegro, C.: Ecommerce, a new way of buying: the case of purchasing fashion items. Dissertation from Instituto Superior de Contabilidade e Administração de Coimbra (2021). http://hdl.handle.net/10400.26/38627

Pereira, C.S.G.: Digital influencers and the behavior of followers on Instagram: An exploratory study [Master's dissertation, ISCAP Intituto Politécnico do Porto]. RCAAP (2017). http://hdl.handle.net/10400.22/11195

Pestana, M., Gageiro, J.: Análise de Dados para Ciências Sociais: A Complementaridade do SPSS, 6ª Edição. Lisboa: Ed. Sílabo (2014)

Pinto, A.F.S.: Digital influencers and the communication of brands acting on blogs and Instagram. Master's thesis, Universidade Fernando Pessoa (2018)

Pontes, A.: Purchase Behavior. In: E-Commerce: Influence of Web Experience (2018)

Rejan, L., Neves, M.F.: Photography and consumption: influence of youth culture on consumer profile, pp.64–71 (1996)

Solomon, M.: Consumer Behavior: Buying, Having, and Being. Person Education, London, UK (2019)

Thaichon, P., Brown, J.R., Weaven, S.: Guest editorial: special issue introduction: E-tailing: the current landscape and future developments. Asia Pac. J. Mark. Logist. 33(6), 1289–1291 (2021)

Upadhyay, Y., Paul, J., Baber, R.: Effect of online social media marketing efforts on customer response. J. Consum. Behav. 21, 554 571 (2022). https://doi.org/10.1002/cb.2031

Wagner, G., Schramm-Klein, H., Steinmann, S.: Online retailing across e-channels and e-channel touchpoints: empirical studies of consumer behavior in the multichannel e-commerce environment. J. Bus. Res. 107, 256–270 (2020)

People-to-Machine
and Machine-to-People

The Man-Machine Relationship on the Web: Motivation to Use the Internet

Jorge Figueiredo[1] (ID), António Cardoso[2] (ID), Margarida Pocinho[3] (ID),
and Isabel Oliveira[1][(✉)] (ID)

[1] Lusíada University, Famalicão, Portugal
`isabel.m.m.oliveira@gmail.com`
[2] University Fernando Pessoa, Porto, Portugal
`ajcaro@ufp.edu.pt`
[3] Polytechnical Institute of Coimbra, Coimbra, Portugal
`margarida_pocinho@estescoimbra.pt`

Abstract. In an environment characterized by turmoil and unpredictability, by the digital transition and transformation, and by the economic and social effects caused by the global public crisis (COVID19), this study aims to analyze the motivations for using the internet and making online purchases, identifying the perceived benefits and consumer satisfaction. For this, an exploratory study with descriptive design was carried out, through the administration of a questionnaire (google forms). 385 consumers responded. The data show that there are significant differences between groups (buyers and non-buyers) in terms of motivation, perceptions of benefits and satisfaction. The use of online shopping platforms fosters a relationship that favors efficiency and enhances feelings of control and freedom in purchasing behavior. The experiences lived through technological intermediation, given the possibility of interaction and personalization, add value to brands, create an innovative identity, while contributing to obtaining a memorable and satisfying experience.

Keywords: Man-machine · Relationship · Web · Motivation · Satisfaction

1 Introduction

Currently, we are witnessing a technological evolution that allows for an expansion and globalization of digital networks, building and spreading through the interconnection of messages, in the context of virtual communities in constant mutation, in a «cyberspace» that breaks with space borders-temporals. There is, in this way, a diversification and simplification of the «interfaces» articulated with the digital phenomenon that flow towards a large-scale adhesion in «cyberspace» with the worldwide interconnection of computers.

In this period of transition and digital transformation, which many authors called the "fourth industrial revolution" or "industry 4.0" [1], new technologies emerge such as

© ICST Institute for Computer Sciences, Social Informatics and Telecommunications Engineering 2023
Published by Springer Nature Switzerland AG 2023. All Rights Reserved
T. Pereira et al. (Eds.): IoECon 2022, LNICST 458, pp. 55–65, 2023.
https://doi.org/10.1007/978-3-031-25222-8_5

the Internet of Things (IoT), Artificial Intelligence (AI), Environments Cyber-physics, Robotics, Sensors, 3D Printing, Big Data, Augmented Reality, cloud computing.

This turbulent, dynamic, volatile, and unpredictable environment [2], was aggravated by the recent global public crisis (COVID-19) that affected the competitiveness of organizations [3]. Digital infrastructure and technologies have been more critical than ever during the Covid-19 crisis. Communication infrastructure and access to the Internet have been strategic in supporting economic and social life. Quarantine has increased the virtualization of economic and social relationships (telework may prevail in more sectors and regions), further accelerating digitization and stimulating investment in automation and robotics, as well as increasing the use of artificial intelligence (AI) tools.

The Internet provides personalized interactivity, and increasingly multimedia, due to its ability to incorporate new combinations of text, images, moving images and sound. It also has an almost unlimited space to offer levels of depth, texture and context, impossible in any other medium. Thus, the company, to customize its information, will have to, when interacting with each audience, acquire detailed and updated information about the customer, to present its content, according to the habits of each user, enabling each one of its consumers, transforming itself into a potential co-creator and intervening customer in the dynamics of the brand and the product.

The Internet imposes itself in the digital context with certain capabilities that are fundamental for the affirmation of different areas, such as Marketing, Advertising or Management. In this sense, multimedia, convergence, synergy and interactivity are the potential that stand out the most in the online phenomenon.

The user interface is the part of an application that is dedicated to dialogue with its user. It is what establishes between man and machine, a relationship of interactivity.

This concept refers to the type of relationship that makes the behavior of one system change the behavior of the other. By extension, a device or a program is interactive when its user can modify its behaviors or developments. While computer software and video games are, by construction, interactive, audiovisual programs and classic films imply passive user behavior [4, 5].

Electrotechnology seems to be evolving according to a feedback process, giving rise to new technologies. And, in fact, it was computers that introduced a series of new interface-relationships between users and screens, contrary to the passive relationship established until then by television, in a mass market by large one-way communication audiences. The computer screen, when inserting bidirectional interactivity modalities, increased the speed, fully immersing the integrated hypermedia [4].

This new communicational support presents its contents in a different way from the conventional means, being able to customize and direct them to each individual of an audience, providing a responsiveness and allowing, therefore, a more effective company-client interactivity.

Faced with this paradigm shift, Internet users will not react in the same way to the interaction facilities that cyberspace provides and to the persuasion that companies do with online consumers. It is pertinent to observe the Man-Machine interaction with regard to motivation and perception regarding the use of the Internet and their online purchase satisfaction.

2 Literature Review

For many multimedia specialists, it is in the transition from analogue to digital video that the key to the success of the New Information and Communication Technologies lies with the public. Some problems arising from analogue media, such as the loss of information quality with distance and the duplication or limitation of expression imposed by this technology, find in digital a greater assimilation of the animated image and sound, by easily inserting purely synthetic images to perform truncations and editing and modulate transmission according to the desired quality, reception conditions and the type of programs [6, 7].

Computers already have the ability to solve numerous tasks that were confined to human thought, with speed and precision that surpass everything that human beings can achieve, fostering a telepresence enabled by communication technologies and projected to the outside world through the connection of computers to the network, stimulating an extreme diversity of media, namely, the ease of access to large national and international files, anywhere and almost instantaneously [8].

In today's society, social networks establish relationships and interactions between individuals of a certain group and enjoy a determining function of spreading information, ideas and influences through Internet communities that encourage their members to share information of common interest. These nuclei have characteristics that are totally different from traditional social groups, which were confined to geographic and temporal proximity [9].

Currently, with the Internet, subjects elect the communities they want to exert their influence there and create a public or semi-public profile and establish contact with users of that network [10].

In addition, online social networking applications allow users to create virtual social networks that facilitate communication through an interactive network, which include user profiles, photos, groups, emails, blogosphere or music, enabling multiple users to join together in a virtual environment [9].

The information society creates a rupture in the paradigm instituted by the industrial society, through the development of the Internet and its platforms, where, in turn, the technological engine determines new models of economic and social organization. It is a society with new rules, structures and patterns of behavior. Emerging forms of business dynamization based on the technological component also appear and revolutionize the way companies and consumers communicate, evolve and market products [11, 12].

The technological phenomenon imposes rapid changes in the pattern of consumption, purchase and commercial offer, in three main areas: in the office, at home and on the move. At the business level, the use of the Internet as a tool for competitive advantage became essential, initially functioning as a communication and relationship support tool in sales, fostering new forms of service provision, with a view to greater customer loyalty. Later, the Internet became part of a fundamental information tool, contributing to greater business productivity [13].

Through the dissemination of information, social networks enhance knowledge and the ability to influence the diffusion of innovation, become a platform for sharing knowledge between social groups, but also become the support for interaction with companies, brands and applications. In this context, Marketing seeks to create empathy with network members, instilling in the group a feeling of commitment, with the aim of arousing interest and sharing of content. In this way, companies see their communication suffer the viral effect and thus reach a large number of recipients per propagation [14].

New digital technologies have imposed certain forms of commercialization on the market, which in turn, develop different online behaviors. These forms of customer relationships on the Internet undoubtedly go through motivations that drive consumers to establish an interactive relationship with companies and their products [15–17].

There is a significant range of studies related to consumer motivations for online shopping that focus exclusively on utilitarian motivations, consolidated by rational shopping experiences. Currently, there is a tendency to also study the phenomenon of emotional satisfaction motivation in the Internet purchase process, such as pleasure, aesthetics, emotion and fun as additional purchase motivations.

It can also be observed that consumers, in line with utilitarianism, are more concerned with purchasing efficiently and without wasting time, which contrasts with the hedonic perspective, with emphasis on the pursuit of pleasure, fun and fantasy. Online utility buyers are looking for a purchase process that favors the performance of the website based on the privileges obtained in view of the fulfillment of the access objective, reflecting its value and the usefulness of the website in solving their needs. This form of relationship seeks efficiency in purchasing and enhances feelings of control and freedom in choosing their products [18, 19].

Hedonic behaviors look for recreational motivation, more attendance, longer duration and propensity to explore the website. The stimuli provided by the research process are as or more important than the purchase of the product, and the greater the recreational component, the greater the positive impact on mood, satisfaction and the possibility of impulsive purchases. The hedonic aspect has, therefore, greater affluence to websites where the customer is continuously motivated and seeks the surprise effect, exclusivity, enthusiasm, socialization/community and involvement [20].

The knowledge of this motivational issue is fundamental for the applicability of persuasive techniques that companies can implement with online consumers, when they use animation and creativity in the creation of the website [21].

Companies promoting motivation in their potential customers in browsing and shopping online also contribute to their trends and respective satisfaction.

Effectively, the ability of brands to exceed expectations is the formula for customer satisfaction, pleasure and loyalty. However, this satisfaction cannot be confined to the product because customers may be satisfied with the products, but not satisfied with the quality of the service provided, or with the price. Furthermore, some studies present satisfaction as a fundamental element for trust [22, 23].

Based on the particularities developed in web shopping, the author [24] show a model developed by Matthew K.O. Lee, who states that, in addition to the differentiating factors of products or services, there are other elements, such as speed and ease of use, essential for consumer satisfaction. Thus, the greater the satisfaction, the greater the appreciation for repeating the experience. The antecedents of satisfaction are confined to the delivery capacity of the products, customer support, price and different features of the website. In addition, the content of the website, the quality and the way in which the products or services are presented, the clarity of the pages, the usefulness of the store, the interactivity with the customer, the convenience of use and the selection of available products are important [25–28].

The role of Experimental Marketing is referred as a process to identify and satisfy the needs and aspirations of customers, promoting reciprocal communication that stimulates the brand's personality and adds value to the segment, creating memorable experiences that generate the buzz/word-of-mouth, renewing the consumer into a prescriber and as a brand promoter [29].

3   Methodology and Sample

The purpose of this article is to analyze the motivations and perceptions of consumers regarding internet use. In this sense, the following research questions were defined:

[Q_1] - Are the motivations for using the Internet related to online shopping?
[Q_2] - What are the perceptions of consumers regarding internet use?
[Q_3] - What is the satisfaction of users with online shopping platforms?

Additionally, it is intended to analyze whether the perceptions of consumers are different in two groups, those who make online purchases and those who do not.

To pursue the objective, a structured questionnaire based on the literature is developed, covering the dimensions "motivation for using the internet", and "satisfaction with online shopping platforms". The pre-test was applied to a convenience sample of 25 respondents, which allowed for some improvements in the layout of the questionnaire, but no changes were made to the main variables. The questionnaire was made available online and data collected between February and May 2021. The answers were given on a Likert scale, ranging from "1" with "totally disagree" to "5" with "totally agree".

The study population consisted of internet users, without any type of restriction. For the calculation of the sample, a margin of error of 5% was defined, resulting in a value of 400 respondents as a representative sample of the universe.

The sample consisted of less than 15 subjects, as they had to be eliminated for not having completed the survey, thus leaving 385 respondents (Table 1) with an average age of 28 years and the majority (58.2%) are women. Most respondents (42.1%) use the internet more than 4 h a day.

It should also be mentioned that 224 of the respondents are students (48.2%) and 57 are professors (14.8%), two groups who use the internet daily and collaborate in research work.

Table 1. General characteristics of the sample

Variables	Attributes	N	%
Sex	Feminine	224	58,2%
	Masculine	161	41,8%
Internet usage	Up to 8 h/week	38	9,8%
	>8 h <20 h/week	185	48,1%
	>4 h/day	162	42,1%
		385	100,0%

4 Analysis and Discussion of Results

The following tables show, for each item to be analyzed, the mean (M) of respondents' responses according to the Likert scale and the respective standard deviation (SD) for online shoppers (Yes) and non-shoppers (No). The Student's T-statistic (t) and the respective degrees of freedom (gl) are also presented, as well as the p-value corresponding to the statistical test of the null hypothesis the mean of the variable being equal to zero (p-value).

Table 2 intends to analyze whether the motivations for using the internet are related to online shopping.

Table 2. Motivation for using the Internet versus online shopping

	Yes (n = 356)		No (n = 29)		t	gl	p-value
	M	SD	M	SD			
– See how people vote or comment on a topic/product	3,22	1,024	3,16	1,120	0,531	383	0,432
– Interact with the website	3,04	1,142	3,07	1,109	1,121	383	0,128
– Discuss or talk about something I saw	3,56	1,125	3,12	1,105	−0,452	383	0,672
– Interact with other people	3,76	1,194	3,75	1,174	−0,563	383	0,254
– Show me	2,07	1,142	2,60	1,187	−1,022	383	0,153
– Vote or comment on a topic	2,93	1,089	2,68	1,205	0,789	383	0,345
Add information to the website	2,82	1,076	2,37	1,167	0,793	383	0,219
– Faster access	3,85	1,107	3,99	1,204	0,843	383	0,395
– Maximize the information I want	3,74	1,106	2,69	1,117	0,867	383	0,236
– Compare prices	3,78	1,115	3,73	1,294	1,099	383	0,157

(continued)

Table 2. (*continued*)

	Yes (n = 356)		No (n = 29)		*t*	*gl*	*p-value*
	M	SD	M	SD			
– Low cost	3,74	1,039	3,45	1,197	0,983	383	0,145
– Search information by topics	3,82	1,043	3,56	1,145	1,521	383	0,122
– Search for information by past affairs	3,65	1,045	2,98	1,278	0,783	383	0,287
– Decide what I want to see	3,28	1,106	2,76	1,188	0,730	383	0,423
– Being able to see several notes or news at the same time	3,73	1,102	3,01	1,637	−0,248	383	0,574
– Be constantly updated	3,65	1,121	3,49	1,123	−0,145	383	0,644

As shown in Table 2, it appears that the motivations for using the internet do not vary significantly with the habit of shopping online or not. It is concluded that in the sample under study, the use of the internet is independent of whether or not respondents make online purchases.

Although there are no differences in the motivations for using the internet and shopping online, it seems important to understand the perception of those who make online purchases (yes) and those who do not (no), regarding the strategies used by Digital Marketing. Table 3 intends to show whether there is a difference in attitudes and trust between those who buy and do not buy via the internet.

Table 3. Consumers' perceptions regarding online purchases

	Yes (n = 356)		No (n = 29)		*t*	*gl*	*p-value*
	M	SD	M	SD			
– Possibility of personalized treatment	3,34	1,072	3,12	1,453	1,541	383	0,121
– Possibility to contact the company	3,67	0,845	3,45	1,291	0,856	383	0,245
– Possibility of being contacted by the company	3,55	0,097	3,37	1,032	1,012	383	0,278
– Possibility to compare prices	3,78	0,874	3,21	1,123	2,423	383	0,023
– Possibility to view the most up-to-date information	4,12	1,023	3,67	1,206	0,873	383	0,234
– Biggest and best offer	3,31	1,023	3,89	1,301	1,194	383	0,132
– Obligation to view content (pop-up, advertising banner)	2,25	1,122	3,21	1,432	−0,987	383	0,328

(*continued*)

Table 3. (*continued*)

	Yes (n = 356)		No (n = 29)		*t*	*gl*	*p-value*
	M	SD	M	SD			
– Shopping online is easy and convenient	2,77	1,021	3,11	1,013	5,410	383	0,001
– I like shopping online	2,99	1,056	2,12	1,123	6,981	383	0,002
– I find it very interesting to shop online	3,28	1,091	2,27	1,302	6,175	383	0,011
– Buying online satisfies my needs	3,64	1,045	2,33	1,221	5,032	383	0,000
– It's exciting to shop online	2,79	1,112	2,67	1,305	2,994	383	0,002
– Buying online is much more fun than in traditional commerce	1,98	1,174	2,23	1,321	1,072	383	0,138
– Shopping online is boring	2,45	1,101	2,54	1,165	−3,482	383	0,008
– Online communication is annoying	2,12	0,973	3,02	1,201	−2,673	383	0,000

It appears that there is a differentiation between online buyers and non-buyers in 8 of the 15 dimensions evaluated. In fact, non-buyers find webmarketing strategies significantly more irritating and annoying than buyers.

The T-student statistic reveals that the motivations did not differ according to the use of the Internet, to buy products or not. Both groups present as a reason for using the Internet the update, the search for information, the maximization of both the information and the news they choose, and the interaction with other people.

Regarding the perceptions of the benefits of online shopping platforms, respondents emphasize "update", "contact", "personalization" and "response to user needs". On the part of non-buyers, they show greater irritability and annoyance with regard to webmarketing strategies.

From the analysis of Table 4 and regarding satisfaction, it appears that there is a differentiation between online buyers and non-buyers, however, despite finding statistically significant differences between "buyers" and "non-buyers", consumers consider themselves satisfied with online purchases, with the services provided and with the usefulness of the portals and platforms for these purchases.

The data obtained in this study are in line with the scientific evidence identified in the literature, as there are favorable motivations for using the internet [30] and the use of online shopping platforms fosters a relationship that privileges efficiency and enhances feelings of control of freedom in purchasing behavior [18, 19].

Furthermore, the experiences lived through technological intermediation, as defended by Smilansky [29] given the possibilities of interaction and personalization [27, 28], add value to brands, create a innovative identity, while contributing to the achievement of a memorable and satisfying experience [15, 17].

Table 4. Satisfaction with online shopping platforms

	Yes (n = 356)		No (n = 29)		t	gl	p-value
	M	SD	M	SD			
– Overall, I am satisfied with my online shopping experiences	3,01	1,023	3,98	1,032	4,765	383	0,002
– I am satisfied with the services (payment, delivery, after-sales, …) of the online stores	3,08	1,036	3,98	1,077	4,739	383	0,003
– I am satisfied with the usefulness of the Internet for my purchases	3,45	0,875	3,02	1,207	5,968	383	0,002

5 Conclusions

Today's society is experiencing a period of transition and digital transformation, where organizations are called to innovate and find new ways of relating to customers. Gradually, the creation of digital business models and the development of portals and online channels, as well as other online tools, allows them to increase their visibility in the market and promote a personalized and interactive relationship with consumers.

The study developed in this investigation allowed the identification of consumer motivations regarding online purchases, highlighting the "capacity for interaction", "collaboration", "autonomy" and "speed". On the other hand, significant differences were found regarding the strategies used by Digital Marketing between those who buy online and those who don't, at the level of "trust" and "consumer satisfaction".

Regarding perceptions of the benefits of online shopping platforms, respondents highlight "updating", "contact", "personalisation" and "response to user needs".

Non-buyers find web marketing strategies significantly more irritating and annoying.

In general, although there are statistically significant differences between "buyers" and "non-buyers", consumers consider themselves satisfied with online shopping, with the services provided and with the usefulness of online shopping portals and platforms.

The study's findings may be of interest to companies that are migrating to digital, as through knowledge of the perceptions of the benefits of online channels and consumer motivations, they can adapt their offer, creating the highest quality, interactive online stores, up-to-date and easy to use. Likewise, recognizing the reasons for resistance to online shopping, they can develop actions that mitigate and reduce these risks, creating conditions for them to start shopping online.

On the other hand, companies that are already exploring online channels and resorting to web marketing can assess consumer satisfaction and, recognizing the factors that contribute to satisfaction, create the conditions for a memorable experience.

However, despite the interest, relevance and implications of the study, the results described here only represent the opinions of the consumers surveyed, making it impossible to generalize the conclusions to the entire population.

It is suggested that in the future the sample of respondents be expanded, the investigation extended to other types of consumers (young and seniors), that gender issues be explored and that a particular sector be focused (for example, banks), as well as consider other dimensions (e.g. recommendation, loyalty).

References

1. Lu, Y.: Industry 4.0: a survey on technologies, applications and open research issues. J. Ind. Inf. Integr. **6**, 1–10 (2017)
2. Mack, O., Khare, A., Krämer, A., Burgartz, T. (eds.): Managing in a VUCA World. Springer, Cham (2016). https://doi.org/10.1007/978-3-319-16889-0
3. Guo, H., Yang, Z., Huang, R., Guo, A.: The digitalization and public crisis responses of small and medium enterprises: Implications from a COVID-19 survey. Front. Bus. Res. China **14**(1), 1–25 (2020). https://doi.org/10.1186/s11782-020-00087-1
4. Kang, J., Lee, J., Jin, S.: Personal sensory VR interface utilizing wearable technology. In: 2018 International Conference on Information and Communication Technology Convergence (ICTC), pp. 546–548. IEEE (2018). https://doi.org/10.1109/ICTC.2018.8539405
5. Nora, D.: Os Conquistadores do Ciberespaço. Editora Terramar, Lisboa (1996)
6. Balan, T., Robu, D., Sandu, F.: Multihoming for mobile internet of multimedia things. Mob. Inf. Syst. **2017**, 1–16 (2017). https://doi.org/10.1155/2017/6965028
7. Monet, D.: O Multimédia. Instituto Piaget, Lisboa (1996)
8. Von Krogh, G.: Artificial intelligence in organizations: new opportunities for phenomenon-based theorizing. Acad. Manag. Discov. **4**(4), 404–409 (2018). https://doi.org/10.5465/amd.2018.0084
9. Tiago, M., Veríssimo, J.: Digital marketing and social media: why bother? Bus. Horiz. **57**(6), 703–708 (2014). https://doi.org/10.1016/j.bushor.2014.07.002
10. Marques, V.: Redes Sociais 360 Como Comunicar Online. Actual Editora, Lisboa (2016)
11. Alahmadi, A.: Always best-connected mobile sensor network to support high accuracy internet of farming. Comput. Eng. Appl. J. **6**(2), 51–58 (2017). https://doi.org/10.18495/comeng app.v6i2.202
12. Dionísio, P., Vicente Rodrigues, J., Faria, H., Canhoto, R., Correia Nunes, R.: B-Mercator, Blended Marketing. Dom Quixote, Alfragide (2013)
13. Fulgoni, G.: Are you targeting too much? Effective marketing strategies for brands. J. Advert. Res. **58**(1), 8–11 (2018). https://doi.org/10.2501/JAR-2018-008
14. Fernandes, S., Belo, A.: Social networks as enablers of enterprise creativity: evidence from Portuguese firms and users. J. Technol. Manag. Innov. **11**(2), 76–85 (2016). https://doi.org/10.4067/S0718-27242016000200008
15. Chen, F., Li, M., Wu, H., Xie, L.: Web service discovery among large service pools utilising semantic similarity and clustering. Enterp. Inf. Syst. **11**(3), 452–469 (2017). https://doi.org/10.1080/17517575.2015.1081987
16. Hellier, P., Geursen, G., Carr, R., Rickard, J.: Customer repurchase intention. Eur. J. Mark. **37**(11/12), 1762–1800 (2003). https://doi.org/10.1108/03090560310495456
17. Ramkumar, B., Woo, H.: Modeling consumers' intention to use fashion and beauty subscription-based online services (SOS). Fashion Text. **5**(1), 1–22 (2018). https://doi.org/10.1186/s40691-018-0137-1
18. Howie, K.M., Yang, L., Vitell, S.J., Bush, V., Vorhies, D.: Consumer participation in cause-related marketing: an examination of effort demands and defensive denial. J. Bus. Ethics **147**(3), 679–692 (2015). https://doi.org/10.1007/s10551-015-2961-1

19. Jeong, M., Lambert, C.: Adaptation of an information quality framework to measure customers' behavioral intentions to use lodging websites. Int. J. Hosp. Manag. **20**(2), 129–146 (2001). https://doi.org/10.1016/S0278-4319(00)00041-4
20. Wolfinbarger, M., Gilly, M.: Shopping online for freedom, control, and fun. Calif. Manag. Rev. **43**(2), 34–55 (2001). https://doi.org/10.2307/41166074
21. Papacharissi, Z., Rubin, A.: Predictors of internet use. J. Broadcast. Electron. Media **44**(2), 175–196 (2000). https://doi.org/10.1207/s15506878jobem4402_2
22. Pham, T., Ahammad, M.: Antecedents and consequences of online customer satisfaction: a holistic process perspective. Technol. Forecast. Soc. Change **124**, 332–342 (2017). https://doi.org/10.1016/j.techfore.2017.04.003
23. Too, L., Souchon, A., Thirkell, P.: Relationship marketing and customer loyalty in a retail setting: a dyadic exploration. J. Mark. Manag. **17**(3–4), 287–319 (2011)
24. Greening, D., Turban, D.: Corporate social performance: as a competitive advantage in attracting a quality workforce. Bus. Soc. **39**(3), 254–280 (2000). https://doi.org/10.1177/000765030003900302
25. Mittal, V., Kamakura, W.: Satisfaction, repurchase intent, and repurchase behavior: investigating the moderating effect of customer characteristics. J. Mark. Res. **38**(1), 131–142 (2001). https://doi.org/10.1509/jmkr.38.1.131.18832
26. O'Sullivan, D., McCallig, J.: Customer satisfaction, earnings and firm value. Eur. J. Mark. **46**(6), 827–843 (2012). https://doi.org/10.1108/03090561211214627
27. Wang, H., Du, R., Olsen, T.: Feedback mechanisms and consumer satisfaction, trust and repurchase intention in online retail. Inf. Syst. Manag. **35**(3), 201–219 (2018). https://doi.org/10.1080/10580530.2018.1477301
28. Ying, S., Bodoff, D.: The effects of web personalization on user attitude and behavior: an integration of the elaboration likelihood model and consumer search theory. MIS Q. **38**(2), 497–A10 (2014)
29. Smilansky, S.: Experiential Marketing - A Pratical Guide to Interactive Brand Experiences. Kogan Page Limited, London (2019)
30. Korgaonkar, P., Wolin, L.: A multivariate analysis of web usage. J. Advert. Res. **39**(2), 53 (1999)

Cybersecurity Challenges in Healthcare Medical Devices

Ana Longras[1]([⊠]) [iD], Teresa Pereira[2] [iD], and António Amaral[3] [iD]

[1] Instituto Politécnico de Viana do Castelo, Viana do Castelo, Portugal
ana.longras@ipvc.pt
[2] Centro ALGORITMI, Universidade do Minho, Guimarães, Portugal
tpereira@dsi.uminho.pt
[3] INESC TEC–Institute for Systems and Computer Engineering, Technology and Science,
4200-465 Porto, Portugal
antonio.m.amaral@inestec.pt

Abstract. Medical devices are rapidly evolving and becoming more interconnected with healthcare networks, overcoming resource constraints, and increasingly focused on patient well-being and needs.

This work intends to identify future research themes in the area of cybersecurity in health by surveying the articles being developed and identifying their current limitations and future work. The developed analysis was based on the publications with the highest number of citations, enabling us to find several challenges and restrictions such as integrating devices in systems.

Innovations and the emergence of new technologies with inherent security vulnerabilities, will continue to evolve, escalating the attackers interest in exploiting unknown cybersecurity risks within healthcare. It is mandatory to consider cybersecurity risks since the conception of the devices to reduce security flaws, ensure the patients with a better quality of life, and guarantee information security properties.

Keywords: Cybersecurity · Medical devices · Healthcare · Review · Vulnerability · Digital transformation

1 Introduction

Medical Device Regulation considers a medical device an instrument, apparatus, appliance, software, implant, reagent, material, or other article is used for any of the following procedures: diagnosis, prevention, monitoring, treatment or alleviation of disease, disability, or injury, but not used for disability or injury prevention [1].

The distinction between a medical device and a device used in the healthcare context is often confused. The rule is clear, any device that is "intended for use in diagnosing disease or other conditions, or in curing, mitigating, treating, or preventing disease" requires Food and Drug Administration (FDA) approval to be a medical device [1].

T. Pereira et al. (Eds.): IoECon 2022, LNICST 458, pp. 66–75, 2023.
https://doi.org/10.1007/978-3-031-25222-8_6

There are approximately 2 million medical devices on the market worldwide [2]. Some can be implanted in patients' bodies called Implantable Medical Devices (IMD) to continuously or automatically treat or deliver one or more medical conditions.

Technological advances provide transformations in the provision of healthcare and also in self-care devices. In practice, it is in healthcare that greater use of wearables is seen more often.

Generally, patient health wearables are considered low risk and not regulated by the FDA as its primary services for general wellness use.

Wearables are self-contained, non-invasive devices that perform a specific medical function, such as monitoring or support over a long time period, aiming to provide a personal medical assistant. Generally, they are equipped with wireless communication capabilities for system/software upgrades, device reconfiguration, data access, and transfer [3].

However, with the advancement of wearable technology, the FDA has regulated some new features. For example, the Apple Heart Study has received FDA approval for the pulse and electrocardiogram function, thus supporting the agency's decision [4].

Additionally, it is available on the market with a wide variety of devices with more and more functionalities, from sleep monitoring, electrocardiogram, oxygen meter, connection to emergency services, and temperature measurement, among others. The 5G network access will provide even more potential with more efficient batteries, use of the cloud, and use of artificial intelligence to support the user with advice or reports that can be shared with medical institutions or health professionals towards facilitating diagnosis and prevention of diseases at a broader distance and more in advance.

The isolation and restrictions resulted from COVID-19 pandemic context has brought positive transformations and opened up a multitude of opportunities for change, accelerating the adoption of digital solutions at a pace never seen before. It led people to monitor their health condition more and has demonstrated the value of eHealth services such as telemedicine and remote patient care. Remote care is here to stay, helping the entire healthcare sector to become increasingly digital and interconnected.

The interconnectedness between all systems and devices in the health sector brought significant contributions to all stakeholders, playing a crucial role in the provision of health care, consequently increasing the life expectancy and providing active aging of the population, with huge impacts on the sustainability of health care systems.

In the meantime, the massive use of devices is not only a positive point, but it has also opened a gap in commitment and guarantee of user safety.

The massive use of devices leads the healthcare sector to face the complexity of systems, the increasing number of connected devices, software and operating systems used on the devices, communication between devices, the transfer and storage of health information, and its regulation. All these elements have inherent security risk vulnerabilities, being exposed to attackers intended to compromise the confidentiality, integrity, and availability of services and data.

The FDA recognizes the safety of medical devices is a shared responsibility among stakeholders, including healthcare facilities, patients, suppliers, and medical device manufacturers.

Failure of cybersecurity protection can result in compromised device functionality, loss of availability or data integrity (medical or personal), or exposure of other connected devices or networks to security threats. This, in turn, can result in the patient's illness, injury, or even in a more dramatic situation into death [5].

This work is organized as follows: Sect. 1 introduces cybersecurity challenges. Section 2 identifies the current state of the art, presenting the different issues on the subject based on the most cited articles. Section 3 consists of identifying and characterizing challenges related to cybersecurity in medical health devices. Section 4 ends with some conclusions from the current challenges of medical devices in healthcare.

2   Literature Review

2.1   Methodology Approach

The research methodology developed was based on a literature review of medical devices used for monitorization and health support and their associated cybersecurity risks supported by a bibliometric analysis using the VOSviewer software [6].

The literature review consisted of analyzing the 20 most cited articles to understand the structure and knowledge research developed by peers, including all types of sources, e.g., conference journals, chapters, etc. The extracted documents were carried out in December 2021 from two knowledge bases, Scopus and Web of Science (WoS).

Search queries defined are followed presented:

- ALL (cybersecurity) OR ALL ("cyber security") AND TITLE-ABS-KEY ("medical device"))
- ALL = (cybersecurity) AND (TI = (medical devices) OR TS = (medical devices) OR AB = (medical devices) OR AK = (medical devices))

The search results were stored in files in "txt" format, including citation information, bibliographic information, abstract and keywords, and other information such as conference and reference information. The objective of confirming all the information was to validate the quality of the sources within the universe of the most cited articles.

Figure 1 shows that in most cited articles, the keyword 'security' was confirmed as expected with the highest number of occurrences. Followed by the keywords 'medical devices' and 'biomedical equipment' with the same number of occurrences. Simultaneously, the keywords 'computer security'; 'embedded systems'; 'implantable medical devices'; 'patient safety'; 'security and privacy', and 'network security' were abundantly mentioned.

There is a wide range of research topics based on the keywords that are present along with cybersecurity and medical devices.

2.2   Literature Review Overview

The literature studied mentions different medical devices from biosensors related to implant devices. Accordingly, to Camera et al. (2015), an implant consists of a sensor

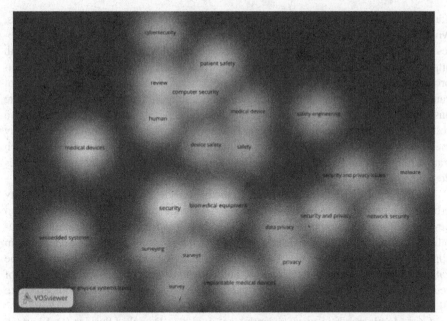

Fig. 1. Keywords of the most cited sources in the area of cybersecurity in health.

or a set of sensors placed inside the human body to monitor any part of it; neurostim-ulators are devices that transmit low-amplitude electrical signals through one or more electrodes placed in different locations in the brain; cardiac devices such as pacemakers and implantable cardioverter defibrillators (ICD) when equipped with telemetry have a radio transmitter that communicates with an external device and sends physiological data, which the healthcare professional can use to detect the patient's pathology [7].

Cybersecurity on medical devices is closely related to cyber-physical systems (CPS), which are systems used to monitor and control the physical world, embedded systems in a network. In medical devices, cyber-physical systems are present in wearables and IMD.

Several authors investigated medical devices regarding the security and privacy of presented CPS. They highlighted the complexity of the CPS identification due to the components' heterogeneity, which introduces difficulties in cybersecurity and privacy protection [8, 9].

Vulnerabilities and Attacks. All assets (physical, digital and human resources) have inherent security vulnerabilities, usually underestimated and exploited by attackers to create critical impacts and gain financial advantage [10]. A recent technical report claims that nearly 10 to 15 networked medical devices are present within a single bed in a hospital [11]. Hence, the interest in the security of networked medical devices has increased, thus increasing the attack reach. The theme most explored by the authors of the most cited articles in the area, is focused on the failures and weaknesses/flaws of medical devices.

The weaknesses are mainly concentrated on the software, which goes from stor-ing credentials, and weak or non-existent authentication to arbitrarily running code. The hardware also has inherent vulnerabilities, which can be exploited, such as on the sensors, where the attacker may interfere with the signal [12]. Most medical devices have wireless communication and, consequently, interferences vulnerabilities, which can result in attacks, noise, eavesdropping, repetition, repetition attacks, and injection attacks, compromising the integrity and availability of the devices. Therefore, one of the recurrent causes is the lack of encryption [8]. Some authors suggest that given the cryptographic hash function and the decentralized nature, several devices need to be protected; as a solution, using blockchain to store data. However, one of the main difficulties of many medical devices is related to energy consumption in a blockchain network, where each transaction needs to be validated, requiring computational power, which some devices do not have [4].

Yaqoob et al. (2019) studied a hundred medical devices to understand cybersecurity problems; identifying hardware, firmware, and software vulnerabilities used in medical devices is of extreme importance since it is responsible for critical functions; vulnerabilities coming from a personal computer or smartphone application; connections from applications to the gateway via Wi-Fi; data stored in the cloud and data storage at the gateway where there may be a lack of authentication and weak encryption; lack of access control to data stored in the cloud; and finally, communication protocols like BLE/Zigbee/Wi-Fi/RF/Ethernet can also be an attack vector [13].

Critical vulnerabilities were recently exploited by a Denial of Service (DoS) attack on millions of connected devices used in hospital networks based on stacks of Nucleus TCP/IP. The attack consists of remote code execution, which allowed attackers to disrupt medical equipment and patient monitors, as well as IoT devices that control systems and equipment in all facilities, such as lighting and ventilation systems, exploits the vulnerability CVE-2021-31886 critical in File Transfer Protocol (FTP) servers does not correctly validate the length of user commands, leading to stack-based buffer overflows that can be used for denial of service and remote code execution [14].

False data injection attack (FDIA) consists of manipulating or altering data intended to inject the same data and losing data integrity [15]. A simple example is a change of a health record, such as the blood type or type of diabetes, which could seriously impact the patient.

Other types of attacks have been mentioned by the authors of the most cited documents in the area, such as the ransomware attack. In May 2021, Ireland's public health service was forced to shut down its information systems due to a ransomware attack. The attack forced several hospitals and clinics to cancel appointments and disrupted the system for tracking contacts and scheduling new vaccines for covid-19 [16].

The 2020 and 2021 years were marked by the COVID-19 pandemic, increasing the wide use and dependence on applications and technological gadgets and, consequently, increasing the number of phishing attacks. Sometimes, a phishing attack is just a mean to materialize a bigger and, more powerful attack. An example that enables us to demonstrate this statement is the cyber-attack that occurred at the University of Florida Health Leesburg Hospital and The Villages Regional Hospital on May 31, 2021, which compromised the electronic health record (EHR), turning them unavailable, and yet not recovered, since the patient care records are still handled by paper. The ultimate goal was a ransomware attack, which exploited the employee's vulnerability through a simple phishing email [17].

Another example of a phishing attack occurred at Saint Agnes Health Care, Inc. of Maryland, by compromising an email account with privileged access. Nearly 25,000 medical records with patient names, dates of birth, medical record numbers, health insurance information, and clinical data were exposed [18].

Solutions. In the literature review, several solutions and proposals were presented to mitigate cybersecurity risks on medical devices.

Pycroft et al. (2018) state that the solutions to IMD's concerns go through 4 cybersecurity recommendations: First, there must be an audit, where there must be detailed records of device activities and access events; second, there must be post-sale surveillance to identify and correct faults quickly; then point out that there are access controls as an access requirement, and finally, make doctors aware of cybersecurity risks [19].

Gollakota et al. (2011) proposed the use of an external device called a "shield" for all communications between IMD and the programmer to limit communications access.

Proximity-based access controls are another proposal, conditioning device communications located within a short distance [20].

The hardware tokens are solutions for the medical team's use as a key to access the devices.

There are still proposals for the use of biometric solutions through the reading of the iris with a near-infrared camera, validating the access identity.

Regarding the devices requiring energy charge, Fei et al. present a CPS-oriented solution to control the physical object to prevent an attacker from guessing the resonant frequency of the energy charge and manipulating the values [21].

Camara et al. (2015) prioritize mechanisms to detect anomalies specifically for implantable medical devices rather than solutions to mitigate threats. If an attack is detected, the patient is notified, or the device is no longer accessible, disconnecting all communications and keeping the medical functions running. Depending on the device, it is devised based on parameters like location, time, day, and the time interval of the same reader action. Based on the activity, the classifier will determine whether it is valid. Each time the reader tries to contact the medical device, it sends a message to the patient's cell phone with the access pattern. The phone runs the sorting algorithm and returns an output which is sent back to the IMD [7].

Some medical devices have highly sensitive information, most often communicated to health professionals. If the information suffers an attack that causes unavailability or compromises its authenticity, it can cause severe consequences for the patient. In this approach presented by Priya et al., it is used a neural network (deep neural network) as a critical solution to increase the efficiency of an Intrusion Detection System (IDS) in cyberattacks' detection [22].

Limitations. The diverse solutions still have limitations or open other points vulnerable to failure in the cybersecurity of medical devices.

The external device proposals assume that the device is not an entry point for exploring the primary device; they assume the external device is trustworthy.

Proposals based on proximity of the calculated distance is less than a fixed limit, communication continues; otherwise, it is interrupted. The main disadvantage of using tokens or biometric solutions is that other solutions have external devices and even at a distance. In an emergency where the healthcare professional needs to access and manipulate the device, it is essential to guarantee its availability and accessibility in person or remotely. Patient safety is always the priority, giving rise to a set of solutions called "Breaking the Glass" (BTG), which consists of allowing all cybersecurity controls to be turned off in a critical event health situation for the patient, thus ensuring the priority is the patient's life. In the meantime, the BTG solution creates an opportunity for the attacker.

The authors in [8] highlight that the devices have to be considered whole. Devices are integrated into a system right from the beginning of the design, and the cybersecurity vulnerabilities of the device must be foreseen in the interaction with other devices and with people. They emphasize the importance of working together between manufacturing, bioengineering, and cybersecurity specialists to ensure that in addition to the devices being functional, the patient is guaranteed the security of data and communications and the privacy of health information.

Although proposed and implemented defense solutions already exist, it is emphasized the need to have further investments in research for CPS cybersecurity flaws, to provide new solutions and respond to the threats and vulnerabilities recently identified and others yet to emerge. The technological advances and the organizations' interest to rapidly turn the products available in the market result, most of the time, in the underestimation of cybersecurity risks, which encourage attackers to exploit their inherent vulnerabilities [9].

One of the many medical device limitations identified by several authors is within the IMD, which has few processing resources, physical size limitations, and battery life. The emergency, where the patient's life is at stake, is highlighted by most cited authors as a clear additional challenge for cybersecurity. The devices cannot be accessible to unauthorized persons; however, in an emergency, they cannot prevent patient care.

The authors in [23] state that the first step to addressing cybersecurity challenges is for organizations to understand the vulnerabilities of networked medical devices, including the exposure of confidential and privacy-threatening information. Followed by the definition of cybersecurity requirements in the design and manufacturing processes and reviewed with the application of standards. Finally, the need to establish cybersecurity responsibility as a requirement in device design is mentioned.

The authors in [24] mention that cybersecurity should be part of the patient care culture. In this context, the patient must be informed and aware of the cybersecurity risks and threats that can compromise the integrity and availability of medical devices.

Although there is research in the field of cybersecurity in medical devices, many patients are unaware of the extent of cyberattacks and the cybersecurity risks that can affect information security properties, namely authentication, integrity, non-repudiation, confidentiality, availability, and authorization [25].

Medical devices are used outside of hospital settings. Depending on the device and procedures, they are used in leisure spaces, in the workplace, and at home, handled by health professionals to lay caregivers. A wide variety of environmental conditions add difficulties to the cybersecurity of devices and patients; for example, there is no way to prevent the user from connecting devices to untrusted networks.

When cybersecurity risks are detected in software, hardware, or any other technology, which can result in a cybersecurity attack, the FDA shares the information with all entities, from manufacturers, healthcare providers, and government agencies, among others, to mitigate manufacturers products' vulnerabilities and find solutions [24].

In short, the most cited sources know the need to involve all areas of design and idealization of medical devices with cybersecurity professionals. They present different proposals with the limitations and implications of the devices and systems inserted. However, the patient's life will always be a priority. The starting point to be considered in investigations is that in case of life or death, cybersecurity rules cannot prevent the assistance of any health professional from assisting the patient.

3 Cybersecurity Challenges

The challenges in the literature focus on mitigating or extinguishing the limitations and attack vectors of the systems.

One of the great challenges of medical devices and the entire healthcare area, consider the interoperability of systems as the key to progress to improve healthcare. Reducing costs and improving clinical decision-making using different information insights. For systems to be interoperable, problems such as: not transmitting or not knowing how to transmit information accurately and securely must be resolved; the need to have or learn how to receive information securely; there is integration and learning how to process and correlate with data from various sources and optimize for the data for the intended purpose, working to maintain the three pillars (confidentiality, integrity, and availability) from the beginning to the end of the life cycle of medical devices.

In addition to the interoperability challenge, cybersecurity has to be seen not as a problem that can be solved but as a risk that everyone involved has an obligation to manage. We predict that cybersecurity attacks on medical devices will continue for the value of health information. We reinforce that there are already some standards such as Health Insurance Portability and Accountability Act (HIPAA), ISO 27000 series, NIST cybersecurity standards, with a lot of documentation, there is no need to invent, and the standards progress and are revised. Notwithstanding, the evolvement of digital literacy between citizens and health professionals will help to reduce the impacts of cybersecurity attacks, as well as to deepen the awareness level of the probable causes of the attacks which globally might reduce the frequency and its impacts.

4 Conclusions

Human life and patient health are priorities and are increasingly dependent on medical systems and devices. The healthcare industry will always be an interesting industry for attackers to exploit cybersecurity flaws.

Many proposals provide a reasonable level of security but require a lot of resources, which is unfeasible given the need to save resources on some of the devices. Alternatively, all technological solutions are often vulnerable to attack as a result of weak or over-priced designs.

Devices must be used responsibly, and users must know various details about their functioning and potential threats to raise awareness to adopt cybersecurity devices' good practices. It is crucial for the users' awareness of cybersecurity policies and good practices because an incorrect behavior can compromise the most sophisticated technological security procedure.

The most cited publications in the cybersecurity health domain focus on communications between devices and third parties, methods of protecting data stored and in transit, access controls, maintenance and updates of device software, incident response, cybersecurity training from patients to healthcare providers, to guarantee the confidentiality, integrity, and availability of information and all medical systems. The future will involve working on better architecture/idealization of solutions implemented across the healthcare sector, working together with healthcare, manufacturing, and cybersecurity specialists.

References

1. MDR - Article 2 - Definitions - Medical Device Regulation (2022). https://www.medical-device-regulation.eu/2019/07/10/mdr-article-2-definitions. Accessed 22 Jan 2022
2. Medical devices. https://www.who.int/health-topics/medical-devices#tab=tab_1. Accessed 05 Jan 2022
3. Feng, L., et al.: Research and application progress of intelligent wearable devices. Chinese J. Anal. Chem. 49(2), 159–171 (2021). https://doi.org/10.1016/S1872-2040(20)60076-7
4. Sneha, S., Panjwani, A., Lade, B., Randolph, J., Vickery, M.: Alleviating challenges related to FDA-approved medical wearables using blockchain technology. IT Prof. 23(4), 21–27 (2021). https://doi.org/10.1109/MITP.2021.3072535
5. FDA.gov (2022). https://www.fda.gov/files/Content-of-Premarket-Submissions-for-Management-of-Cybersecurity-in-Medical-Devices---Guidance-for-Industry-and-Food-and-Drug-Administration-Staff.pdf. Accessed 05 Jan 2022
6. VOSviewer - visualizing scientific landscapes. https://www.vosviewer.com/. Accessed 28 Feb 2022
7. Camara, C., Peris-Lopez, P., Tapiador, J.E.: Security and privacy issues in implantable medical devices: a comprehensive survey. J. Biomed. Inform. 55, 272–289 (2015). https://doi.org/10.1016/j.jbi.2015.04.007
8. Humayed, A., Lin, J., Li, F., Luo, B.: Cyber-physical systems security—a survey. IEEE Internet Things J. 4(6), 1802–1831 (2017). https://doi.org/10.1109/JIOT.2017.2703172
9. Hossain, M., Islam, S.M.R., Ali, F., Kwak, K.S., Hasan, R.: An Internet of Things-based health prescription assistant and its security system design. Future Gener. Comput. Syst. 82, 422–439 (2018). https://doi.org/10.1016/J.FUTURE.2017.11.020
10. Pereira, T., Barreto, L., Amaral, A.: Network and information security challenges within Industry 4.0 paradigm. Procedia Manuf. 13, 1253–1260 (2017). https://doi.org/10.1016/J.PROMFG.2017.09.047
11. Fierce Healthcare: 82% of healthcare organizations have experienced an IoT-focused cyberattack, survey finds. https://www.fiercehealthcare.com/tech/82-healthcare-organizations-have-experienced-iot-focused-cyber-attack-survey-finds. Accessed 22 Feb 2022
12. Rushanan, M., Rubin, A.D., Kune, D.F., Swanson, C.M.: SoK: security and privacy in implantable medical devices and body area networks. In: 35th IEEE Symposium on Security and Privacy (SP 2014), pp. 524–539 (2014). https://doi.org/10.1109/SP.2014.40

13. Yaqoob, T., Abbas, H., Atiquzzaman, M.: Security vulnerabilities, attacks, countermeasures, and regulations of networked medical devices-a review. IEEE Commun. Surv. Tutor. **21**(4), 3723–3768 (2019). https://doi.org/10.1109/COMST.2019.2914094

14. NVD - CVE-2021-31886 (2021). https://nvd.nist.gov/vuln/detail/CVE-2021-31886. Accessed 14 Feb 2022

15. Ahmed, M., Pathan, A.S.K.: False data injection attack (FDIA): an overview and new metrics for fair evaluation of its countermeasure. Complex Adapt. Syst. Model. **8**(1), 1–14 (2020). https://doi.org/10.1186/S40294-020-00070-W/FIGURES/7

16. ABC News: Ireland's health service hit by "significant" ransomware attack. https://abcnews. go.com/International/irelands-health-service-hit-significant-ransomware-attack/story?id= 77685241. Accessed 22 Jan 2022

17. Cyberattack Drives 2 UF Health Hospitals to EHR Downtime. https://healthitsecurity.com/ news/cyberattack-drives-2-uf-health-hospitals-to-ehr-downtime. Accessed 22 Jan 2022

18. Saint Agnes Health Care Hack Exposes 25,000 HIPAA Records. https://www.hipaajour nal.com/saint-agnes-healthcare-hack-exposes-25000-hipaa-records-5663/. Accessed 22 Jan 2022

19. Pycroft, L., Aziz, T.Z.: Security of implantable medical devices with wireless connections: the dangers of cyber-attacks. Expert Rev. Med. Devices **15**(6), 403–406 (2018). https://doi. org/10.1080/17434440.2018.1483235

20. Gollakota, S., Hassanieh, H., Ransford, B., Katabi, D., Fu, K.: They can hear your heartbeats: non-invasive security for implantable medical devices. SIGCOMM Comput. Commun. Rev. **41**(4), 2–13 (2011). https://doi.org/10.1145/2043164.2018438

21. Hu, F., et al.: Robust cyber-physical systems: concept, models, and implementation. Future Gener. Comput. Syst. **56**, 449–475 (2016). https://doi.org/10.1016/j.future.2015.06.006

22. Swarna Priya, R.M., et al.: An effective feature engineering for DNN using hybrid PCA-GWO for intrusion detection in IoMT architecture. Comput. Commun. **160**, 139–149 (2020). https:// doi.org/10.1016/j.comcom.2020.05.048

23. Williams, P.A., Woodward, A.J.: Cybersecurity vulnerabilities in medical devices: a complex environment and multifaceted problem. Med. Devices (Auckland, N.Z.) **8**, 305–316 (2015). https://doi.org/10.2147/MDER.S50048

24. Coventry, L., Branley, D.: Cybersecurity in healthcare: a narrative review of trends, threats and ways forward. Maturitas **113**, 48–52 (2018). https://doi.org/10.1016/j.maturitas.2018.04.008

25. Patients Unaware of the Extent of Healthcare Cyberattacks and Data Theft. https://www.hip aajournal.com/patients-unaware-of-the-extent-of-healthcare-cyberattacks-and-data-theft/. Accessed 25 Feb 2022

26. Cybersecurity|FDA: https://www.fda.gov/medical-devices/digital-health-center-excellence/ cybersecurity#safety. Accessed 25 Feb 2022

A WSN Real-Time Monitoring System Approach for Measuring Indoor Air Quality Using the Internet of Things

Elias Biondo[1,2], Thadeu Brito[3,4,5](), Alberto Nakano[1],
and José Lima[3,5]

[1] Federal University of Technology - Paraná, Toledo, Brazil
eliasbiondo@alunos.utfpr.edu.br, nakano@utfpr.edu.br
[2] Polytechnic Institute of Bragança, Bragança, Portugal
[3] Research Centre in Digitalization and Intelligent Robotics (CeDRI), Instituto Politécnico de Bragança, Campus de Santa Apolónia, 5300-253 Bragança, Portugal
{brito,jllima}@ipb.pt
[4] Faculty of Engineering, University of Porto, Porto, Portugal
[5] INESC TEC - INESC Technology and Science, Porto, Portugal

Abstract. Indoor Air Quality (IAQ) describes the air quality of a room, and it refers to the health and comfort of the occupants. Typically, people spend around 90% of their time in indoor environments where the concentration of air pollutants and, occasionally, more than 100 times higher than outdoor levels. According to the World Health Organization (WHO), indoor air pollution is responsible for the death of 3.8 million people annually. It has been indicated that IAQ in residential areas or buildings is significantly affected by three primary factors, they are outdoor air quality, human activity in buildings, and building and construction materials. In this context, this work consists of a real-time IAQ system to monitor thermal comfort and gas concentration. The system has a data acquisition stage, captured by the WSN with a set of sensors that measures the data and send it to be stored on the InfluxDB database and displayed on Grafana. A Linear Regression (LR) algorithm was used to predict the behavior of the measured parameters, scoring up to 99.7% of precision. Thereafter, prediction data is stored on InfluxDB in a new database and displayed on Grafana. In this way, it is possible to monitor the actual measurement data and prediction data in real-time.

Keywords: Indoor Air Quality · Monitoring System · Internet of Things · Wireless Sensor Network

1 Introduction

In some cases, people may spend around 90% of their time, mainly at home or in the workplace, indoor environment conditions contribute significantly to human well-being [1]. According to the World Health Organization (WHO), the Indoor

T. Pereira et al. (Eds.): IoECon 2022, LNICST 458, pp. 76–90, 2023.
https://doi.org/10.1007/978-3-031-25222-8_7

Air Pollution (IAP) is responsible for the death of 3.8 million people annually [2]. Harmful pollutants inside buildings include, but are not limited to, carbon monoxide (CO), carbon dioxide (CO_2), Volatile Organic Compounds (VOC), Particulate Matter (PM), aerosols, and biological pollutants [3].

Some of the reasons behind poor air quality are ventilation, building materials, human activities, and repeated use of chemical-rich products that are responsible for CO, CO_2, VOCs, O_3, NO_2 and SO_2 concentration in indoors environments [4]. In a specific case of human activities, the CO_2 concentration in enclosed spaces increases according to the number of people (due to human beings exhaling CO_2). Higher CO_2 concentrations can cause nausea, dizziness, vomiting, reduction of cognitive function, headaches, and fatigue [4]. Moreover, VOCs' concentrations in indoor environments are at least ten times higher than outdoors, regardless of the building location. Furthermore, VOCs are considered to be harmful risks to human health and potentially cause cancer in long-term exposure [5].

Indoor Air Quality (IAQ) is often not prioritized due to distraction of people during the performance of their activities throughout the day or there may also be a loss of perception/sensitivity of the smell when people get used to the air during breathing, among other factors. However, these indoor environments can become intelligent and alert critical air quality levels. The alert can be obtained by monitoring the gases present in the indoor air compositions through sensors. Spreading sensors in a given internal space can identify possible elevations of the parameters that are distributed in the internal space. In this way, people could be warned that the environment must be aerated, for example, opening a window. This approach could be a possible solution to guarantee the air quality of internal spaces and, consequently, the well-being of the people present in the environment.

Based on air quality and risks that this can cause to people's health if it is not controlled, this work presents a system development capable of monitoring the IAQ using a Wireless Sensor Network (WSN). The developed WSN is comprised by modules with sensor that must measure parameters that influence the air quality. Then, the WSN must send the data to a database that can be accessed by a monitoring platform, showing the air quality during periods such as days, weeks or months.

The rest of the paper is organized as follows. After the introduction, Sect. 2 presents the related work. In Sect. 3, the system architecture is addressed to describe each part (hardware and software) of the proposed approach. An example of the final prototype module and its circuit is exhibited in Sect. 4. After, in Sect. 5, the WSN is stressed with some tests to validate the proposed acquisition data. The last section, Sect. 6, concludes the paper and points out some direction for future work.

2   Related Work

Monitoring indoor environments through sensor modules involve many technologies and methodologies because several sensors are capable of operating indoors to detect parameters for determining the IAQ index. The IAQ monitoring requires a specific selection of sensors and communications protocols. For example, the work in [6] shows that IAQ is dependent on several thermal comfort parameters, especially temperature and humidity. In the same way, some of the gases and substances for IAQ analyses are CO_2, CO, VOC, and NOx and the MQ series sensors are known for cost-effective measurements of gases in the indoor environment [7]. However, MQ135 is highlighted as a multi-gas sensor for IAQ measurements being capable of measuring many different parameters such as CO_2, benzene (C_6H_6), ethanol (C_2H_5OH), NOx, ammonia (NH_3), and smoke [8]. According to [9], the BME680 sensor is widely recommended for measuring VOC, atmospheric pressure, humidity, and temperature. To monitor formaldehyde (CH_2O) levels, the ZE08-CH_2O sensor is used in some research [10].

When using sensors in monitoring systems, WiFi is one of the most preferred choices [11], because it is available in most buildings (different to systems developed by [12,13]). To transfer data to the dedicated server from the target site, several researchers work with Message Queuing Telemetry Transport (MQTT) protocol for its ability to support easy implementation and low power consumption [14]. For example, the device developed in [15] is a prototype of monitoring system for IAQ designed to use MQTT protocol to send the data, measured by MQ135 and DHT11 sensors, to a cloud data storage. Another example can be seen in [16], where the air quality of a classroom is related to the concentration of O_2, CO, CO_2 and NH_3 gases with MQ135, MG811, MQ7 and ME2O2 sensors. Other facility monitored by sensor is demonstrated in [17] which developed a low-cost device with BME680 and CCS811 sensors to monitoring some IAQ parameters in a hospital. In the same way, [18] developed a low-cost Internet of Things (IoT) device with BME680 and CCS811 sensors and ESP32 microcontroller equipped with WiFi communication systems that monitors the temperature, humidity, equivalent dioxide carbon (eCO_2), and TVOC. The collected data is stored on the database platform InfluxDB [19]. The microcontroller ESP32 have been used in a lot of researches for IAQ Monitoring, making available some useful functionalities, such as WiFi and Bluetooth communication, in addition to low-power consumption [20].

3   System Architecture

The IAQ monitoring system through a WSN in this work involves combining several hardware and software tools. For a better understanding of the whole system, Fig. 1 illustrates a block diagram representing a high-level integration of the system. The system is separated into two main parts, the first is the hardware architecture, which is responsible for sensing all the gases parameters and executing the communication with the cloud and the second is the software architecture, which stores and processes the data received by the hardware.

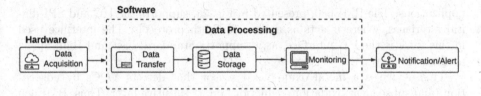

Fig. 1. Phases of implementation process of an IAQ monitoring system.

3.1 Hardware

The proposed system has individuals modules to make the data acquisition process, accordingly, it is possible to perform the monitoring at several points in the same environment or even in different spaces. Each module's hardware contains an ESP32 microcontroller and three gas sensors, the MQ135, the BME680, and the ZE08-CH2O (Fig. 2). The choice of these devices was based on IAQ monitoring studies presented in [15,17,18]. Moreover, the modules' design is expected to consider the cost-benefit ratio.

The choice of ESP32 was due to the lower power consumption and the WiFi integration allows a large physical range and direct connection to the Internet via a router [21]. Other sensors, such as DHT11, MQ5, MQ7, and CCS811, were tested before obtaining this configuration. On the other hand, all four sensors presented less stability and precision during the breadboard test. Also, they were more expensive than the chosen sensors. In this context, the main characteristics of each sensor of the module responsible to measure the IAQ parameters will be presented below.

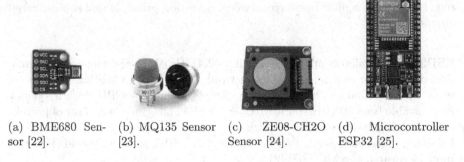

(a) BME680 Sensor [22].   (b) MQ135 Sensor [23].   (c)   ZE08-CH2O Sensor [24].   (d)   Microcontroller ESP32 [25].

Fig. 2. Set of sensors inserted in each WSN's module.

BME680. It is a digital 4-in-1 sensor with gas, humidity, pressure and temperature measurement based on proven sensing principles [22]. This sensor is widely used in IAQ, IoT, home automation, monitoring systems, and weather forecast applications. The BME680, presented in Fig. 2a, supports the I^2C and SPI digital interfaces, where it acts as a slave for both protocols. The interface used in this work is the I^2C interface, as it supports Standard, Fast and High-Speed modes.

This device is a metal oxide-based sensor that detects VOCs by adsorption (and subsequent oxidation/reduction) on its sensitive layer. Thus, BME680 reacts to the most volatile compounds polluting indoor air. In contrast to the sensor's selectivity for one specific component, this sensor can measure the sum of VOCs/contaminants in the surrounding air. This enables BME680 to detect, e.g., outgassing from paint, furniture, and garbage, high VOC levels due to cooking, food consumption, exhaled breath, and sweating [22]. The signal provided by the BME680 sends resistance values inversely proportional to the VOC concentrations present in the environment, the higher the VOCs concentration, the lower the resistance value and vice versa [22].

MQ135. It is a low-cost sensor with tin dioxide (SnO_2) as a sensitive material (Fig. 2b), which has lower conductivity in clean air. When there is a target polluting gas, the sensor conductivity increases proportionally to the gas concentration, for that reason, it is applicable in air quality control equipment for buildings. This sensor is sensitive to some gases, such as NH_3, NO_x, alcohol, C_6H_6 and CO_2 [23].

ZE08. It is a general-purpose and miniaturization electrochemical formaldehyde detection module, demonstrated by Fig. 2c. It utilizes the electrochemical principle to detect methanol (CH_2O). It is sensitive to alcohol, CO, and smoke in the air with significant stability. Moreover, it has a built-in temperature sensor to make compensation and simultaneously provide a digital and analog voltage output. It combines a mature electrochemical detection principle and sophisticated circuit design.

ESP32. This microcontroller is a single 2.4 GHz WiFi-and-Bluetooth combo chip designed for mobile, wearable electronics, and IoT applications. There are two CPU cores that can be individually controlled, and the CPU clock frequency is adjustable from 80 MHz to 240 MHz [26]. ESP32 integrates a rich set of peripherals, ranging from capacitive touch sensors, Hall sensors, SD card interface, Ethernet, high-speed Serial Peripheral Interface (SPI), Inter-IC Sound (I^2S) and Inter Integrated Circuit (I^2C) [21].

3.2 Software

Data processing is done by a set of tools and software (Arduino IDE, MQTT protocol, Node-RED, InfluxDB, Grafana and PyCharm) commonly used for monitoring systems [15,27,28]. Figure 3 shows the phases of this process.

Fig. 3. Software diagram of the system.

The data transfer is responsible to receive the data with Arduino IDE and send to influxDB using MQTT protocol through Node-RED platform. Then, the stored data is sent to Grafana to be monitored and accessed by machine learning algorithm developed on Pycharm.

4 Prototype

Once the group of sensors that will be inserted in each module of the WSN is chosen, it is necessary to perform the circuit diagram. Each sensor has their particularities about the inputs and outputs, interface of communication protocol and power supply. The connection of the sensors with ESP32 is presented in Fig. 4.

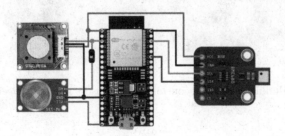

Fig. 4. Circuit connection between ESP32 and each sensor.

Starting with the connection between ESP32 and MQ135, the Vcc pin is connected to 5 V of the ESP32 board, and the ground pin is connected to the ESP32 ground. The analog pin of the MQ135 is connected to the A0 pin of the ESP32 via a resistor. For this sensor, the A0 port is used, this GPIO allows receiving the analog signal from the sensor without WiFi usage interference (WiFi uses analog pins to run). But GPIOs' ESP32 requires a signal with 3.3 V (not 5 V tolerant). A resistor is added between the MQ135 analog pin and the ESP32 A0 pin to protect the GPIOs port from voltage damage.

BME680 outputs resistance values react according to the gas concentration, which means the output signal variation is inversely proportional to the gas concentration. The sensor is connected to ESP32 via I^{2}C communication protocol that uses two wires to share information. The sensor is powered with 3.3 V, and the SDA and SCL outputs are connected to GPIO21 and GPIO22, respectively, which is the default connection I^2C using ESP32.

This ZE08 sensor uses only three pins to connect with the microcontroller, and this device gives an output signal in a range of 0 to 5 ppm with high sensitivity (up to 0.01 ppm). Pins 3 and 4 are GND and VCC, respectively, and Pin 2 of ZE08 is connected to the Vcc pin of ESP32. As well as MQ135, this sensor gives measurement through an analog signal.

After assembling everything in a printed circuit board (PCB), the circuit was enclosed in a box. Figure 5 shows the final result of the module with the microcontroller and sensors responsible for the system's data acquisition stage. Three modules were assembled (Module 1, Module 2, and Module 3).

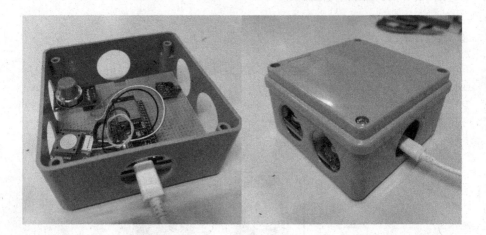

Fig. 5. Module with microcontroller and sensors used to collect data.

5   Results

Each module of Fig. 5 was programmed to collect and store data every two minutes. In Fig. 6, the database of parameters measured in a laboratory of the Institute Polytechnic of Bragança (IPB) is presented graphically. It is noted that from the date 12/20/21 to 01/10/22, the concentration of gases showed levels below average due to the pause in academic activities at the IPB lab due to year-end and new year's period, which reduced human activities in the laboratory.

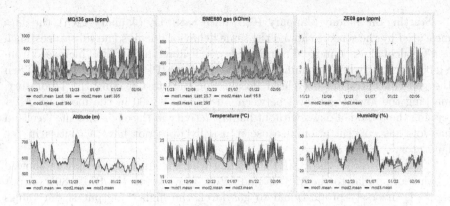

Fig. 6. Temporal graphs of data stored in the database.

After some days, it is possible to understand the behavior of these parameters on regular days during a week of activities at IPB's lab. The data stored from January 16th to 23th is presented in Fig. 7. The top graph shows the gas concentration measured by MQ135 and ZE08 sensors over the week, where Module 1 (mod1) is presented in blue, Module 2 (mod2) is orange and Module 3 (mod3) is the green indicator. In bottom graph, only mod1 is not shown since this module does not have the ZE08 sensor.

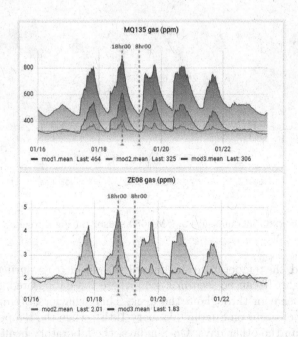

Fig. 7. Gas measure of MQ135 and ZE08 sensors during a week. (Color figure online)

Starting on Sunday (January 16th) until Saturday (January 22th), the data measured by the sensors showed the same behavior due to some substances, such as CO, alcohol, and smoke. From Monday to Friday, the gas level increased from 8 h 00 morning, when the human activities start on IPB's lab, until 18 h 00. Then the gas concentration decreased because people start leaving the laboratory, marking the lowest gas level between 7 h 00 and 8 h 00 in the morning. After passing the period of dawn without human activity in the environment. Weekend has low gas concentration because it usually does not have activities in the laboratory.

Figure 8 presents the BME680 reading where the gas concentration showed a behavior similar to the MQ135 and ZE08. However, as the BME680's output signal is inversely proportional to gas level, the highest output signal values were stored during the dawn period and on weekends (when the lowest levels of the pollutant in the environment are expected). Still comparing BME680 with MQ135 and ZE08, the opposite happens in the morning and afternoon from Monday to Friday. The higher the registered gas level, the lower the values of the BME680 output signal.

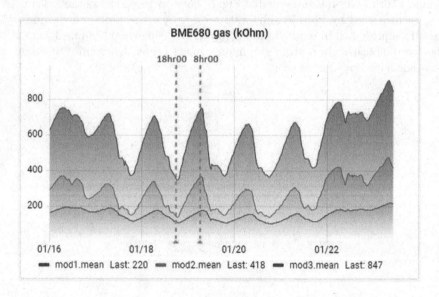

Fig. 8. Gas measure of BME680 sensor during a week.

As expected, the temperature and humidity levels increase during the day and decrease at night. It can be seen in Fig. 9, where the data stored demonstrates the expected behavior throughout the week. This behavior of temperature and humidity did not occur on Sunday (January 16th), when the temperature registered lower than the other days. On Sundays, the laboratory heating system is not turned on.

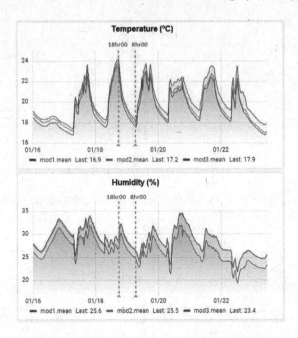

Fig. 9. Temperature and humidity measure of BME680 sensor during a week.

5.1   Forecasts Tests

Using data from January 16th to 23th, an LR algorithm was used to predict the parameters values and the results are presented in Fig. 10. The red line is the actual data used to training the model, the blue line the prediction data resulted from LR model and the grey line represents the error between the two values.

When analyzing the test and the prediction, the error value is close to zero for all tested values where the assertively of BME680 gas concentration (Fig. 10.A) was 99.7%, and the mean absolute error to this prediction was about 1.67 kΩ. Figure 10.B shows the forecast from the gas level registered by MQ135. As well as BME680 gas, LR prediction presented a high assertively degree (95.81%) and about 1.4 ppm of mean error. The prediction of ZE08 gas in Fig. 10.C is similar to MQ135 and scored 95.5% of predict precision and 0.015 ppm of mean error. The score precision of temperature prediction in Fig. 10.D was 99.1%, and the humidity score was 96.7%. In this test, a dataset was used where the parameters did not present changes in behavior to verify the degree of assertiveness of the machine learning model developed. The linear regression model showed a higher degree of precision to predict the data in all cases.

Another test will be presented when changes in gas concentration are disturbed with a combustion simulation. A smoke test was carried out on February 10th so that the sensors could read high concentrations of different gases. In the combustion simulation, a piece of burnt paper was placed next to the modules and they were covered with a box (reducing the air volume to intensify the sen-

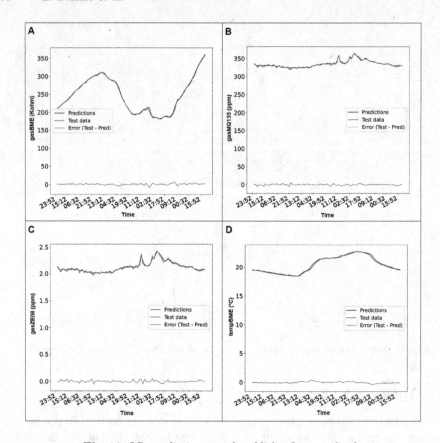

Fig. 10. LR predictions results. (Color figure online)

sor read). The test was carried out for one hour and only the gas levels were changed, while temperature and humidity maintained the same behavior.

The algorithm was run using the test data, as expected, the prediction showed different values from the measured data. Analyzing the Fig. 11.A, the forecast of BME680 gas concentration presents high differences between test and prediction values. The final prediction from LR scored 60.63% and the average error was around 46.33 kΩ. Figure 11.B presents the MQ gas forecast, when analyzing the Error line, it is noted that the measured gas value has values greater than 1500 ppm than the predicted value. The assertively to LR model was 46.61% and the mean absolute error scored around 629.42 ppm. The same behavior happens with ZE08 gas predict, in Fig. 11.C the Error line shows the difference between test and prediction values to the linear regression, the predict in this test was 47.24% and a median error from around 6.5 ppm.

In general, the smoke test presented expected results, given that the learning models were trained to predict the value of gases at normal levels according to the data stored in InfluxDB. This high value of detected error makes it possible to perceive situations that compromise the IAQ of the environment, thus being able to alert, in real time, about variations in parameters.

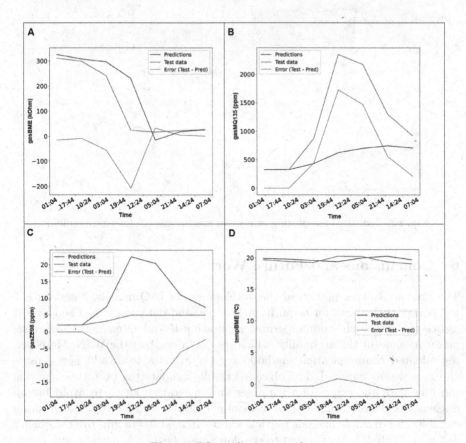

Fig. 11. RL predictions results.

5.2   Real-Time Monitoring

With the trained learning models, the real-time monitoring implementation is done in Grafana with a new database to store prediction values resulted from the LR model. Figure 12 is the real-time monitoring in normal conditions done on March 4th, the measured parameters are highlighted in blue are presenting a behavior similar to predictions values in yellow.

The data read by the sensors is sent to the database and automatically loaded into PyCharm IDE to be used in the learning algorithms, then the prediction values are sent to NodeRED and stored in a database. Then the data is displayed on Grafana to verify that the parameters read are as expected. The entire process is repeated every two minutes to keep monitoring as up-to-date as possible for possible data variations.

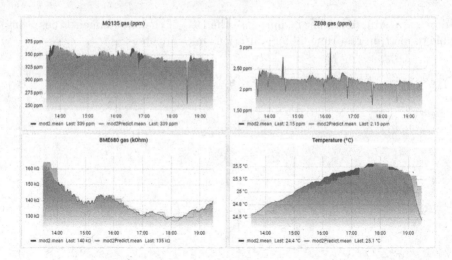

Fig. 12. Real-time monitoring in normal conditions. (Color figure online)

6   Conclusions and Future Work

The presented paper addressed the development of IAQ models, based on IoT technology that allows for acquisition, storage, and data analysis. The low cost associated with each module permits replicating it and spreading it in several places to monitor the air quality, which results in creating the WSN. Moreover, the adopted communication methodology (WiFi) is able to add new sensors and modules as required. The obtained results validate the prototype showing the user with the acquisition variables and generating alerts to avoid breath diseases. As future work, the improvement of modules with more data acquisition variables, for example, include particle sensors in modules to improve the quality of data collected. It is expected to develop an application to control any device focused to solve problems given an alert provided by algorithms predictions. In this sense, adding new prediction algorithms (such as Neural Networks, or a comparison between Supervised and Unsupervised algorithms) are promising directions to follow.

Acknowledgements. Supported by organization FCT - Fundação para a Ciência e Tecnologia within the R&D Units Project Scope: UIDB/05757/2020, and Thadeu Brito was supported by FCT PhD grant SFRH/BD/08598/2020.

References

1. Leech, J., Nelson, W.C., Burnett, R.T., Aaron, S.D., Raizenne, M.E.: It's about time: a comparison of Canadian and American time-activity patterns†. J. Expo. Anal. Environ. Epidemiol. **12**, 427–432 (2002)
2. WHO. Household air pollution and health. https://www.who.int/en/news-room/fact-sheets/detail/household-air-pollution-and-health. Accessed 14 Jan 2022

3. Kumar, P., Imam, B.: Footprints of air pollution and changing environment on the sustainability of built infrastructure. Sci. Total Environ. **444**, 85–101 (2013). https://doi.org/10.1016/j.scitotenv.2012.11.056. https://www.sciencedirect.com/science/article/pii/S0048969712014829

4. Choi, M., et al.: Design and implementation of IoT-based HVAC system for future zero energy building. In: 2017 IEEE International Conference on Pervasive Computing and Communications Workshops (PerCom Workshops), pp. 605–610 (2017). https://doi.org/10.1109/PERCOMW.2017.7917631

5. Tran, V.V., Park, D., Lee, Y.C.: Indoor air pollution, related human diseases, and recent trends in the control and improvement of indoor air quality. Int. J. Environ. Res. Public Health **17**(8) (2020). https://doi.org/10.3390/ijerph17082927. https://www.mdpi.com/1660-4601/17/8/2927

6. Li, J., Yin, S.W., Shi, G.S., Wang, L.: Optimization of indoor thermal comfort parameters with the adaptive network-based fuzzy inference system and particle swarm optimization algorithm. Math. Probl. Eng. **2017** (2017). https://doi.org/10.1155/2017/3075432. https://www.hindawi.com/journals/mpe/2017/3075432/#abstract

7. Saini, J., Dutta, M., Marques, G.: Sensors for indoor air quality monitoring and assessment through internet of things: a systematic review. Environ. Monit. Assess. **193**(2), 1–32 (2021)

8. Alexandrova, E., Ahmadinia, A.: Real-time intelligent air quality evaluation on a resource-constrained embedded platform. In: 2018 IEEE 4th International Conference on Big Data Security on Cloud (BigDataSecurity), IEEE International Conference on High Performance and Smart Computing, (HPSC) and IEEE International Conference on Intelligent Data and Security (IDS), pp. 165–170 (2018). https://doi.org/10.1109/BDS/HPSC/IDS18.2018.00045

9. Folea, S.C., Mois, G.D.: Lessons learned from the development of wireless environmental sensors. IEEE Trans. Instrum. Meas. **69**(6), 3470–3480 (2020). https://doi.org/10.1109/TIM.2019.2938137

10. Russi, L., Guidorzi, P., Pulvirenti, B., Semprini, G., Aguiari, D., Pau, G.: Air quality and comfort characterisation within an electric vehicle cabin. In: 2021 IEEE International Workshop on Metrology for Automotive (MetroAutomotive), pp. 169–174 (2021). https://doi.org/10.1109/MetroAutomotive50197.2021.9502853

11. Firdhous, M., Sudantha, B., Karunaratne, P.: IoT enabled proactive indoor air quality monitoring system for sustainable health management. In: 2017 2nd International Conference on Computing and Communications Technologies (ICCCT), pp. 216–221 (2017). https://doi.org/10.1109/ICCCT2.2017.7972281

12. Zorawski, M., Brito, T., Castro, J., Castro, J.P., Castro, M., Lima, J.: An IoT approach for animals tracking. In: Pereira, A.I., et al. (eds.) OL2A 2021. CCIS, vol. 1488, pp. 269–280. Springer, Cham (2021). https://doi.org/10.1007/978-3-030-91885-9_19

13. Brito, T., et al.: Optimizing data transmission in a wireless sensor network based on LoRaWAN protocol. In: Pereira, A.I., et al. (eds.) OL2A 2021. CCIS, vol. 1488, pp. 281–293. Springer, Cham (2021). https://doi.org/10.1007/978-3-030-91885-9_20

14. Naik, N.: Choice of effective messaging protocols for IoT systems: MQTT, CoAP, AMQP and HTTP. In: 2017 IEEE International Systems Engineering Symposium (ISSE), pp. 1–7 (2017). https://doi.org/10.1109/SysEng.2017.8088251

15. Hapsari, A.A., Junesco Vresdian, D., Aldiansyah, M., Dionova, B.W., Windari, A.C.: Indoor air quality monitoring system with node.js and MQTT application. In:

2020 1st International Conference on Information Technology, Advanced Mechanical and Electrical Engineering (ICITAMEE), pp. 144–149 (2020). https://doi.org/10.1109/ICITAMEE50454.2020.9398324

16. Muladi, M., Sendari, S., Widiyaningtyas, T.: Real time indoor air quality monitoring using internet of things at university. In: 2018 2nd Borneo International Conference on Applied Mathematics and Engineering (BICAME), pp. 169–173 (2018). https://doi.org/10.1109/BICAME45512.2018.1570509614

17. Lasomsri, P., Yanbuaban, P., Kerdpoca, O., Ouypornkochagorn, T.: A development of low-cost devices for monitoring indoor air quality in a large-scale hospital. In: 2018 15th International Conference on Electrical Engineering/Electronics, Computer, Telecommunications and Information Technology (ECTI-CON), pp. 282–285 (2018). https://doi.org/10.1109/ECTICon.2018.8619934

18. Kadir, A.D.I.A., Alias, M.R.N.M., Dzaki, D.R.M., Din, N.M., Deros, S.N.M., Haron, M.H.: Cloud-based IoT air quality monitoring system. In: 2021 26th IEEE Asia-Pacific Conference on Communications (APCC), pp. 121–127 (2021). https://doi.org/10.1109/APCC49754.2021.9609897

19. Influxdata. https://www.influxdata.com/. Accessed 18 Aug 2021

20. Moharana, B.K., Anand, P., Kumar, S., Kodali, P.: Development of an IoT-based real-time air quality monitoring device. In: 2020 International Conference on Communication and Signal Processing (ICCSP), pp. 191–194. IEEE (2020)

21. Espressif Systems: Esp32-wroom-32 datasheet. https://www.espressif.com/sites/default/files/documentation/esp32-wroom-32_datasheet_en.pdf. Accessed 03 Apr 2022

22. Bme680 low power gas, pressure, temperature & humidity sensor. https://cdn-shop.adafruit.com/product-files/3660/BME680.pdf. Accessed 03 Apr 2022

23. Mq135 semiconductor sensor for air quality. https://www.tme.eu/Document/2578fa81c261e398e9967a2f575c3ebe/MQ135.pdf. Accessed 03 Apr 2022

24. Electrochemical ch2o detection module. https://www.winsen-sensor.com/d/files/PDF/Gas%20Sensor%20Module/Formaldehyde%20Detection%20Module/ZE08-CH2O%20V1.0.pdf. Accessed 03 Apr 2022

25. MOUSER ELECTRONICS - ESP32. https://pt.mouser.com/ProductDetail/EspressifSystems/ESP32DevKitC32UE?qsGedFDFLaBXFguOYDKoZ3jA%3D%3D. Accessed 15 Feb 2022

26. Esp32 series datasheet. https://www.espressif.com/sites/default/files/documentation/esp32_datasheet_en.pdf. Accessed 03 Apr 2022

27. Yang, X., Yang, L., Zhang, J.: A WiFi-enabled indoor air quality monitoring and control system: the design and control experiments. In: 2017 13th IEEE International Conference on Control Automation (ICCA), pp. 927–932 (2017). https://doi.org/10.1109/ICCA.2017.8003185

28. Hapsari, A.A., Hajamydeen, A.I., Vresdian, D.J., Manfaluthy, M., Prameswono, L., Yusuf, E.: Real time indoor air quality monitoring system based on IoT using MQTT and wireless sensor network. In: 2019 IEEE 6th International Conference on Engineering Technologies and Applied Sciences (ICETAS), pp. 1–7 (2019). https://doi.org/10.1109/ICETAS48360.2019.9117518

Scalability of IoT Systems: Do Execution Costs Predict the Quality of Service?

Ahmed Al-Qasmi[1], Huda Al Shuaily[1], Kennedy E. Ehimwenma[2(✉)],
and Safiya Al Sharji[1]

[1] University of Technology and Applied Sciences, Al Khuwair 33, PC113 Muscat,
Sultanate of Oman
{ahmed.alqasmi,huda.alshuaily,safiya.alsharji}@utas.edu.om
[2] College of Science and Technology, Wenzhou Kean University, Wenzhou, China
kehimwen@kean.edu

Abstract. Execution costs are broadly used in the evaluation of the scalability of IoT systems. A well-known concern in their use is the extent to which their scalability desiderata best predicts Quality of Service (QoS). At first, past studies did not ratify a relationship between the scalability approaches and QoS in IoT systems. More recently, however, the correlations between these have begun to emerge. In this paper, we extend those findings and open up new avenues to further research by proposing a statistical testing approach for scrutinizing this relationship. The initial findings delineate that there is a significant correlation between the scalability approach employed and QoS in IoT systems. Our results strengthen the use of execution costs in the scalability of IoT systems confirming that QoS can be successfully predicted.

Keywords: Execution costs · Quality of service · Scalability · System performance

1 Introduction

The evaluation of IoT systems has a well-established process in experimental design, with some currently common metrics including latency, packet loss indicators, jitter, bandwidth, and throughput, which are generally used for optimization of network performance [1]. While every organization is constantly seeking QoS when adopting its information systems; it can be presumed that the QoS measured by using these metrics at the default level of the system's configuration will predict the actual QoS in practice. The performance of IoT systems [2], referred to as QoS in this paper, can thus typically be quantified using measures derived from a number of computing services including cloud computing, be it IaaS (Infrastructure as a Service), PaaS (Platform as a Service) or SaaS (Software as a Service), which might all affect the scalability of the IoT systems.

The concept of scalability is crucial to ensure adequate IoT systems since such systems are characterized by an excessive increase in the number of connected things to

© ICST Institute for Computer Sciences, Social Informatics and Telecommunications Engineering 2023
Published by Springer Nature Switzerland AG 2023. All Rights Reserved
T. Pereira et al. (Eds.): IoECon 2022, LNICST 458, pp. 91–100, 2023.
https://doi.org/10.1007/978-3-031-25222-8_8

deal with billions of services. Scalability is defined as the measure of a system's ability [3, 4] to increase or decrease in its performance and cost with respect to changes in the applications and/or system processing demands. As such, it is a metric that expresses how a system's performance is maximized without any degradation in the QoS it provides when additional bandwidth is needed as a consequence of an increase in the load-handling capacity requirement. This will ensure a certain level of performance which might be quantitatively measured when evaluating the network QoS model. For this reason, one might presume that the overall goal of scalable solutions is thus to enhance the QoS.

There are actually two approaches to increase the load-handling capacity of IoT systems: the vertical scalability (or scale-up) approach and horizontal scalability (scale-out) approach. Scale-up solutions are normally characterized by a large symmetric multiprocessing system that shares memory in the same machine. This handles the whole load when it is increased, by using a more powerful computer. Scale-out solutions, on the other hand, are characterized by the usage of smaller clusters of machines. Each machine works with its own operating system. Decades ago, the vertical approach was the most dominant, prior to the horizontal approach becoming widespread due to high-throughput web applications [5]. The current study substantiates a relationship between these two approaches to identify which one is more suitable for the expansion of IoT systems.

Much research in the evaluation of IoT systems has focused on improving the above-mentioned measures, which often assume that, during the analysis of throughput against the bandwidth [3–6], any throughput that is significantly lower than the bandwidth is an indication of a poor network performance. However, this kind of evaluation has been criticized by a number of researchers [1, 15, 21, 22] because the characteristics of the measures used do not pertain to the scalability approaches of IoT systems. This paves the way for a new direction in the evaluation of IoT systems towards the use of execution costs as a measure in determining the relationship between the scale-up and scale-out approaches employed in IoT systems to quantitatively measure their performance. This is important because as [6] assert, the real issue in adopting IoT systems is not whether latency and packet loss indicators are high and low respectively by a statistically significant percentage, but rather whether the execution cost is relatively low in these systems.

This study aims to build upon, and expand, the existing knowledge as to whether or not execution costs are applicable for predicting the scalability of IoT systems and consequently their QoS in terms of performance. We describe a scenario of a smart educational institute equipped with smart surveillance cameras, smart energy management, smart lighting and smart water quality monitoring. No doubt this institute would require additional bandwidth on an as-needed and when-needed basis (e.g., to deploy a highly reliable ANPR solution for smart gate security); this means that the existing infrastructure has to be able to support any increasing number of connected devices, application features, and users, in other words, it must be able to dynamically scale as and when the network requires changes to its topology. Previous research [5, 7–9, 19] into scalability has been conducted, but these studies did not focus on the extent to which in such environments, scaling up (vertical) and scaling out (horizontal) approaches are reliable. However, it is important to adopt the appropriate scaling approach so that the overall performance is maximized without any degradation in the QoS. To the best of our knowledge, this study is the first of its kind to identify the performance of IoT systems using the statistical variance of execution costs to compare the extent to which scale-up and scale-out approaches vary in scaling the IoT systems. This strengthens the use of execution costs in the evaluation of the scalability of IoT systems, confirming that the QoS of IoT systems can be successfully predicted based on the scalability approach adopted.

The remainder of this paper is structured as follows: in the following section, we describe the related literature on system scalability and QoS in IoT systems, while Sect. 3 elaborates on the correlation between the scaling approaches and QoS in IoT systems along with the details of our experimental setup. Section 4 discusses the results from our experiments, and Sect. 5 considers the implications of our findings for the evaluation of IoT systems. We present our proposal for future work and conclude the paper in Sect. 6.

2 Literature Review

The work found in the literature review regarding the most effective scalability approach that best predicts Quality of Service (QoS), is limited. An evaluation mechanism for service composition mechanisms was proposed in [9]; their research however, focused on the review and evaluation of these mechanisms which fall under the umbrella of scalability, but a major limitation of their approach lies in the lack of quality metrics for dynamic reconfiguration to add value to the quality of their functional scalability desiderata. The research study by [10] also provided a major contribution to this field. They used the MapReduce application, which allows the offloading of the computation and communication portions of a scale-up implementation, from the cores of a chip-multiprocessor to their accelerators. While they included a valuable contribution and demonstrated how their hardware-based solution was highly scalable, they did not provide the full range of optimized design aspects.

White et al. [11] conducted a comprehensive study related to QoS for IoT systems in which three different aspects of QoS are discussed: (1) the types of research conducted in the field; (2) the factors of quality being measured; (3) the layers of the IoT architecture. By providing a correlation between scalability approaches, the current study extends the last aspect of this study, in which only consolidated high-level quality characteristics are provided.

Recently, in the field of IoT systems, researchers have also shown an interest in QoS measurements. For instance, the work of Singh et al. [12] categorized QoS measurements by their quality characteristics as three main types including, the QoS of computing, the QoS of things, and the QoS of communication. However, despite the fact that the term metrics is employed in this work, their study focuses on quality characteristics rather than on the formulas which actually define QoS metrics. A few more metrics are discussed by these authors in [13] in the area of wireless sensor networks.

Finally, Staron et al. [14] examined the metrics of the Quality of System architecture including the number of interfaces, the number of coupled components and changes in the architecture per time unit; yet, this study provides a discussion of the metrics which are generally applied in the IoT environment rather than the quality of end devices. However, the research by both [5] and [15] delineated the results of their investigation of the scalability approach that outperforms IoT systems scalability approaches, but the authors did not sufficiently elaborate their experimental set up for further research. In the current study, we have followed a different experimental approach which indicated that the scale-out approach yields a better result by reducing the cost of execution in the cloud; which is also consistent with the results found in both [5] and [15].

3   Methodology

In devising the methodology, we wanted to utilize the cloud execution costs metric to gauge the performance of the two scalability approaches for an IoT system based on a PaaS platform of our smart educational institute. Such an environment is inferred to have similar settings in all devices it is equipped with, including cloud computing required for the full deployment of the IoT system as specified by the cloud service provider. In past experiments, evaluation of IoT systems was performed by coding a simulation of that environment whereby various flexible and scalable java classes provided by the CloudSim package were employed.

However, the set-up costs of these experiments are costly in nature as they require specific code to be applied through each application program; to provide a more controlled experiment, it is preferable to use cloud simulators as they enable quantitative measurement of the systems' performance (i.e. a low execution cost) under different scenarios rather than merely measuring the instruction execution speed. For details about simulators, the reader is referred to [20], the scope of this study is to tackle the QoS problem from the overall perspective of an IoT system to compare the scale-up and scale-out approaches. As such, this scope is a delimitation of our study and we do not focus specifically on QoS metrics. Thus, the overview provided in this paper does not focus either on the quality metrics of specific code or on the criteria for general testing coverage.

3.1   Testing the Scalability Approach

The scale-out approach used in this study is conceptualized in eight different configurations in eight different locations (which we call scenario 1 for our scale-up approach) with one main configuration (scenario 2 for the scale-up approach) at the high-end of each configuration [15], without forcing all solutions into a single setup. We hypothesize that when additional bandwidth is required on an as-needed and when-needed basis, the scale-up or scale-out approach will provide the same QoS for the same specification setup of computing devices; this null hypothesis H_0, can then statistically be interpreted as:

"when an additional bandwidth is required in the network infrastructure, there is no significant difference in the mean of the execution costs with respect to the scalability approach adopted".

In this paper, we use simulation represented in the two scenarios mentioned above, which involve different aspects of the cloud (network, storage, memory, CPU) for our smart educational institute to validate its early stage evaluation rather than adopting real-world testbeds which are both more complex and more expensive [2]; Furthermore, we use the default configurations of the system since these provide the data members which define the bandwidth, RAM, MIPS (million instructions per seconds) and the size of the architecture [1]. We then extract the execution costs in terms of the system's Response Time (RT) and the data center Processing Time (PT), from both the scale-up and scale-out approaches. With these measures, we were able to investigate the correlation between the scale-up and scale-out approaches. In this section, we outline the experimental set up in which we used the default configurations of our IoT systems provided by the service provider in comparing these approaches based on similar architecture.

3.2 Simulation Configurations

The simulated cloud computing for these experiments consists of different configurations equipped with several hosts in each configuration, where one large host representing the scale-up approach, is of greater capability than all other hosts, used for the scaling out approach. For each approach, if we name our eight different configurations as top1, top2, top3, top4, top5, top6, top7 and top8, assuming that each configuration is modelled with the large host, we can use this large host for testing the scale-up approach so that we do not compare apples with oranges. This allows each location to have eight different configurations top1-top8 for the scaling out approach, including one large host which is modelled from the total specifications of the scaling out approach [15].

CloudAnalyst [16][1], an open-source simulator – chosen because of its popularity and capability of simulating tasks requiring flexibility and sophisticated reconfigurability in addition to continuously allowing the experiments to be repeated - was then configured at each host. Since Facebook is a large scaled application that could benefit from the cloud, it was then used for our simulation as workload input, to scrutinize the behaviour of such an application under different deployment configurations. A table of the details of the parameter configurations of our experiment set up of the system (at 1/10th of the scale of Facebook) is elaborated in the appendix along with the distribution of the application by all users (collected on January 15th, 2022) at each user base (top1-top8). It is worth noting that the application was simulated during the peak hours[2] for a total of 60 h [18].

4 Results and Analysis

This section is divided into two parts: 1) the QoS based on the scalability (scale-up and scale-out) approach and 2) the analysis of the results from varying levels of the scalability approach.

4.1 QoS Using Scale-Up and Scale-Out Approach

Assuming that the above application is deployed in each host based on the configurations (top1 to top8) detailed in the appendix, the output results of the simulations in these

---

[1] https://www.opensourceforu.com/2016/11/best-open-source-cloud-computing-simulators/ Last Accessed on 15/Jan/2022.

[2] https://www.omantel.com/ Last Accessed on 10/Jan/2022.

series of experiments are shown in Table 1. Using a paired t-test, a statically significant difference in QoS (execution costs – both the response time in milliseconds – ms - and the processing time in milliseconds) between the two approaches is also illustrated in Table 2 and 3. From Table 1, it is clear that, using the scale-out approach, the execution costs were reduced as compared to the execution costs required in the scale-up approach. These results are further graphically depicted in Fig. 1. The spikes in both the response time and the processing time can be seen clearly with the highest points for the top1 configuration while the lowest points are mostly obtained with more powerful hardware configurations (top8).

Table 1. Execution costs in scale-up and scale-out approaches

	Scale-Up		Scale-Out	
	RT(ms)	PT(ms)	RT(ms)	PT(ms)
top1	274.48	82.47	220.20	40.29
top2	238.70	101.47	255.98	88.56
top3	173.35	48.15	155.05	39.32
top4	174.42	48.10	157.92	39.95
top5	120.24	23.45	101.74	15.65
top6	147.06	21.95	127.60	13.52
top7	113.62	22.62	96.22	12.65
top8	110.57	17.46	92.55	10.66

4.2 Differences Between Scale-Up and Scale-Out Approaches

The observed significant differences in the scalability approaches in IoT systems is probably due to the large difference - shown in Table 2 and 3 - in the execution costs between the scale-up and scale-out approaches. Here, we reduce the gap between the execution costs of scale-up and scale-out approaches to determine the impact on the system's performance (the QoS). The gap reduction is achieved by deducting [17] the execution costs values of the system using the scale-out approach from the scale-up approach (absolute difference), and then sorting the obtained results by the lowest differences in execution costs (Table 2 and 3 delineates the outputs results based on response time and processing time respectively). For the sake of consistency (with top6, see appendix), these outputs are normalized to equal the size set of users of the simulated application. The attribute StaSigDif used in Table 2 and 3, indicates whether or not there exists a statistically significant difference between the two scalability approaches. This allows us to detect when this significant difference in execution costs between scale-up and scale- out approaches disappear. We observe that both tables have significant differences (using a paired t-test), except in top5 for both RT and PT.

Table 2. Absolute difference in scaling approaches (RT)

	top1	top2	top3	top4	top5	top6	top7	top8
Scale-Up	163.45	234.70	124.59	144.63	85.76	147.06	91.77	91.82
Scale-Out	131.13	251.69	111.44	130.95	75.95	127.60	77.72	76.85
StaSigDif	0.00**	0.02*	0.00**	0.00**	0.13	0.03*	0.00**	0.02*

** $p < 0.01$, * $p < 0.05$

Table 3. Absolute difference in scaling approaches (PT)

	top1	top2	top3	top4	top5	top6	top7	top8
Scale-Up	49.11	99.77	34.61	39.88	17.51	21.95	18.27	14.58
Scale-Out	23.99	87.08	28.26	33.13	11.68	13.52	10.22	8.85
StaSigDif	0.01**	0.00**	0.00**	0.00**	0.15	0.04*	0.01**	0.02*

** $p < 0.01$, * $p < 0.05$

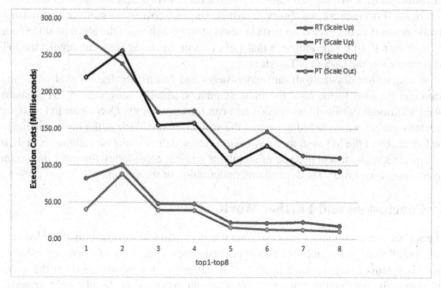

Fig. 1. Graphical representation of execution costs in scale-out and scale-up approaches

5 Discussion

Many research studies previously investigated the important problem of quality metrics (see Sect. 2) for dynamic reconfiguration of the IoT systems, which means reducing the execution costs in these systems. A few of these studies employed simulation approaches without using statistical variance of execution costs, and struggled to establish a significant correlation between the scalability approach employed and the QoS in IoT systems.

In a later study [15] some relationship problems started to be tackled. Following a different approach from earlier research, the current study has distinctively addressed the same issue and provided further evidence to analyze this phenomenon.

Moreover, as far as execution costs are concerned, it is normally expected that they are reduced using a large host (more powerful RAM) rather than a small host (less powerful RAM) and our findings demonstrated a consistency with this common fact. Nonetheless, our experiments showed that variations in simulations performed at different locations based on a large host modelled from the total specifications of smaller hosts, behaved differently and discerned differences between pairs of IoT systems having a tiny absolute difference in execution costs. In other words, costs are significantly ($p < 0.00$) reduced for the IoT scalability in the scale-out approach than in the scale-up approach, indicating a correlation between the scaling approaches and QoS in IoT systems. However, this correlation is reliable only if specific codes are deployed since scalability is context-dependent [15], as demonstrated in previous studies.

From our experiment, we also observe that with large hosts, this correlation is not always more effective, as shown in both top2 (RT and PT) and top6 (RT only) as compared to top1 (RT and PT) and top5 (RT only) respectively. The reason for the lack of correlation in this case is an issue to be addressed and we leave this as an open research question for further studies. We suggest further experiments with real-time monitoring and users' experience. Furthermore, we observe also that execution costs in the scale-out approach is always lower than the execution costs in scale-up approach when the absolute difference is larger than (0.01). This indicates that variations in execution costs can predict the IoT performance or the QoS in IoT systems.

A conclusion drawn from our experiments and results obtained is that execution costs can be used to measure the most suitable scalability approach in IoT systems when additional bandwidth is needed and can thus predict the QoS of an IoT system. Previous studies which failed to predict the scalability approach as the most suitable in the expansion of the IoT systems, may have conducted the simulation techniques in their experiments with inaccurate type of simulator without considering the most important layer – hardware layer - for dynamic reconfiguration of the system.

6 Conclusions and Further WorK

The application of statistical tests used in our experiment to the evaluation of our hypothesis, has allowed us to reject our null hypothesis; we conclude that for the expansion of the IoT systems, using the scale-up approach may not be as beneficial as using the scale-out approach. We demonstrated that the scale-out approach is slightly more effective compared to the scale-up approach. A critical analysis to identify the reason behind the effectiveness of the scale-out approach as compared to the scale-up approach is another open research question. Furthermore, despite using the CloudAnalyst simulator, we do not argue that these results are exhaustively replicable since we did not focus specifically on QoS metrics in our experiments. Thus, the overview provided in this paper focuses neither on quality metrics of specific code nor on the criteria of general test coverage, which could form part of future studies.

However, preference as to whether the scale-up or scale-out approach is well-suited for the scalability of a system is context-dependent, therefore, using these experiments as a starting point, we believe that researchers can design more scalability metrics and more effective evaluation experiments. We have used the statistical variance of execution costs to compare the extent to which scale-up and scale-out approaches vary in scaling the IoT systems. Our study has implications for hardware resources and computing services for the scalability of the IoT systems. Our future work includes modelling framework tools for simulation rather than just using them for evaluation purposes, in addition to incorporating a failure handling mechanism into the simulation. We have learnt that simulation experiments have rich potential in identifying and experimenting with effective measures in the scalability of IoT systems. Unfortunately, due to time constraints, we did not extract the execution costs in terms of hosts utilization and power consumption, which could be beneficial metrics to measure the QoS in IoT systems.

Appendix

Default Configurations in Simulation.

Parameter	Value used
top1 (502,003 users)	4 GB total (from 1 small host modelled with 4 GB RAM)
top2 (304,050 users)	8 GB total (from 2 small hosts modelled with 4 GB RAM each)
top3 (415,952 users)	12 GB total (from 3 small hosts modelled with 4 GB RAM each)
top4 (360,534 users)	16 GB total (from 4 small hosts modelled with 4 GB RAM each)
top5 (400,453 users)	20 GB total (from 5 small hosts modelled with 4 GB RAM each)
top6 (298,952 users)	24 GB total (from 6 small hosts modelled with 4 GB RAM each)
top7 (370,119 users)	28 GB total (from 7 small hosts modelled with 4 GB RAM each)
top8 (360,017 users)	32 GB total (from 8 small hosts modelled with 4 GB RAM each)
Processing Speed	10000 MIPS (Host)
Transmission Rate	1.54 Mbps
Bandwidth (MB)	10000
Cloud latency	100 ms

References

1. Gross, T.R., Hennessy, J.L., Przybylski, S.A., Rowen, C.: Measurement and evaluation of the MIPS architecture and processor. ACM Trans. Comput. Syst. **6**(3), 229–257 (1988)
2. Jain, R.: The Art of Computer Systems Performance Analysis. John Wiley & Sons, Hoboken (2008)
3. Sun, X., Ansari, N.: Edge IoT: mobile edge computing for the internet of things. IEEE Commun. Mag. **54**(12), 22–29 (2016)
4. Li, L., Li, S., Zhao, S.: QoS-aware scheduling of services-oriented internet of things. IEEE Trans. Ind. Inform. **10**(2), 1497–1505 (2014)

5. Michael, M., Moreira, J.E., Shiloach, D., Wisniewski, R.W.: Scale-up x scale-out: a case study using nutch/lucene. In: IEEE International Parallel and Distributed Processing Symposium, pp. 1–8 (2007)

6. Taniuchi, Y.: On-demand virtual system service. Fujitsu Sci. Tech. J **46**(4), 420–426 (2010)

7. Misra, P.: Build a scalable platform for high-performance IoT applications. Technical report, TCS Experience Certainty (2016)

8. Sarkar, C., SN, A.U.N., Prasad, R.V., Rahim, A., Neisse, R., Baldini, G.:. DIAT: a scalable distributed architecture for IoT. IEEE Internet Things J.**2**(3), pp.230–239 (2014)

9. Arellanes, D., Lau, K.K.: Evaluating IoT service composition mechanisms for the scalability of IoT systems. Future Gener. Comput. Syst. **108**, 827–848 (2020)

10. Addisie, A., Bertacco, V.: Collaborative accelerators for in-memory mapreduce on scale-up machines. In: Proceedings of the 24th Asia and South Pacific Design Automation Conference, pp. 747–753 (2019)

11. White, G., Nallur, V., Clarke, S.: Quality of service approaches in IoT: a systematic mapping. J. Syst. Softw. **132**, 186–203 (2017)

12. Singh, M., Baranwal, G.: Quality of service (QOS) in internet of things. In: IEEE 3rd International Conference on Internet of Things: Smart Innovation and Usages (IoT-SIU), pp. 1–6 (2018)

13. Snigdh, I., Gupta, N.: Quality of service metrics in wireless sensor networks: a survey. J. Inst. Eng. (India): Series B **97**(1), 91–96 (2014). https://doi.org/10.1007/s40031-014-0160-6

14. Staron, M., Meding, W.: A portfolio of internal quality metrics for software architects. In: Winkler, D., Biffl, S., Bergsmann, J. (eds.) SWQD 2017. LNBIP, vol. 269, pp. 57–69. Springer, Cham (2017). https://doi.org/10.1007/978-3-319-49421-0_5

15. Rahman, F.H., Au, T.W., Shah Newaz, S.H., Haji Suhaili, W.S.: A performance study of high-end fog and fog cluster in iFogSim. In: Omar, Saiful, Haji Suhaili, Wida Susanty, Phon-Amnuaisuk, Somnuk (eds.) CIIS 2018. AISC, vol. 888, pp. 87–96. Springer, Cham (2019). https://doi.org/10.1007/978-3-030-03302-6_8

16. Wickremasinghe, B., Calheiros, R.N., Buyya, R.: CloudAnalyst: a cloudsim-based visual modeller for analysing cloud computing environments and applications. In: IEEE 24th International Conference on Advanced Information Networking and Applications, pp. 446–452 (2010)

17. Turpin, A., Hersh, W.: User interface effects in past batch versus user experiments. In: 25th Annual International Conference ACM SIGIR Conference on Research and Development in Informational Retrieval, pp. 431–434 (2002)

18. Jena, S.R., Ahmed, Z.: Response time minimization of different load balancing algorithms in cloud computing environments. Int. J. Comput. Appl. **69**(17), 22–27 (2013)

19. Luntovskyy, A., Globa, L.: Performance, reliability and scalability for IoT. In: IEEE International Conference on Information and Digital Technologies (IDT), pp. 316–321 (2019)

20. Bahwaireth, K., Tawalbeh, L., Benkhelifa, E., Jararweh, Y., Tawalbeh, M.A.: Experimental comparison of simulation tools for efficient cloud and mobile cloud computing applications. EURASIP J. Inf. Secur. **2016**(1), 1–14 (2016). https://doi.org/10.1186/s13635-016-0039-y

21. Karakus, M., Durresi, A.: A scalability metric for control planes in software defined networks (SDNs). In: IEEE 30th International Conference on Advanced Information Networking and Applications (AINA), pp. 282–289 (2016)

22. Lilja, D.J.: Measuring Computer Performance: A Practitioner's Guide. Cambridge University Press, Cambridge (2005)

Machine-to-Machine

Transient Session Key Derivation Protocol for Key Escrow Prevention in Public Key Infrastructure

Vincent Omollo Nyangaresi[1], Zaid Ameen Abduljabbar[2,3], Ismail Yaqub Maolood[4], Mustafa A. Al Sibahee[5,6], Junchao Ma[5(✉)], and Abdulla J. Y. Aldarwish[2]

[1] Faculty of Biological and Physical Sciences, Tom Mboya University, 40300 Homabay, Kenya
vnyangaresi@tmuc.ac.ke

[2] Department of Computer Science, College of Education for Pure Sciences, University of Basrah, Basrah 61004, Iraq
{zaid.ameen,abdullajas}@uobasrah.edu.iq

[3] Shenzhen Institute, Huazhong University of Science and Technology, Shenzhen 518118, China

[4] Department of Information and Communication Technology Center (ICTC) – System Information, Ministry of Higher Education and Scientific Research, Erbil, Iraq
ismail.maulood@mhe-krg.org

[5] College of Big Data and Internet, Shenzhen Technology University, Shenzhen 518118, China
{mustafa,majunchao}@sztu.edu.cn, mustafa.alsibahee@iuc.edu.iq

[6] Computer Technology Engineering Department, Iraq University College, Basrah, Iraq

Abstract. The Internet of Things (IoT) devices have been deployed to realize smart environments such as smart cities, smart homes, smart health and smart grids. In these domains, the IoT devices collect and forward high volumes of sensitive and private data. It is therefore important that security schemes be developed to protect the exchanged data. In this regard, a myriad of authentication protocols have been developed over the recent past. However, these schemes deploy cryptographic primitives that result in extremely high communication, storage and computation complexities. In addition, some of these protocols still have numerous security and privacy issues that render them unsuitable for deployment in an IoT environment. For instance, untraceability, anonymity, key escrow problems and attack vectors such as de-synchronization and forgery attacks are frequently ignored. In this paper, a transient session key derivation protocol is developed to address some of these security and efficiency challenges. The security analysis executed shows that this protocol offers untraceability, device anonymity and perfect forward key secrecy. In addition, it is robust against de-synchronization, known secret key leakage, eavesdropping and forgery attacks. In terms of operational efficiency, this protocol incurs the lowest computation and communication complexities.

Keywords: Authentication · De-synchronization · Key escrow · Security · Privacy

© ICST Institute for Computer Sciences, Social Informatics and Telecommunications Engineering 2023
Published by Springer Nature Switzerland AG 2023. All Rights Reserved
T. Pereira et al. (Eds.): IoECon 2022, LNICST 458, pp. 103–116, 2023.
https://doi.org/10.1007/978-3-031-25222-8_9

1 Introduction

In typical cyber physical systems, a number of smart devices are interconnected to form an Internet of Things (IoT). These smart devices collect a myriad of data from their surroundings and then forward the same to some central data servers where processing is accomplished. After some manipulations, transformations and analysis, the collected data can facilitate various activities [1]. For instance, IoT can be amalgamated with cloud computing to realize smart cities [2]. Apart from smart cities, IoT deployments have been utilized to improve healthcare, transportation, safety, efficiency and convenience [3]. Over the recent past, Device-to-Device (D2D) communication has been developed, in which IoT devices exchange messages directly amongst themselves. This helps to offload the servers [4] in addition to boosting reliability and transmission rates. As such, the IoT devices can still communicate even when the central cloud has failed.

Although D2D comes with many benefits, security and privacy of the devices as well as data present some challenges [5, 6]. This is attributed to the numerous vulnerabilities and risks occasioned by device heterogeneity. Consequently, the architectures and protocols utilized in these smart devices are different and incompatible. Since privacy and security implementations in these devices differ, interoperability is also difficult. Therefore, a single privacy and security technique may not be satisfy the requirements of all devices and applications. Ultimately, upholding security and privacy of exchanged data as well as data at rest presents some challenges [7]. Considering smart health IoT systems, sensitive and private information is being generated and transmitted. Compared with wired communication systems, wireless transmissions in IoT is susceptible to many threats and attacks such as eavesdropping, forgery and modifications. Although the interconnectivity among numerous devices brings forth user convenience, this inadvertently increases the attack surfaces. As such, security and privacy among the interconnected devices has become a significant issue [8].

In wireless networks, authentication is normally the first step towards security and privacy preservation [2, 9]. Indeed, the authors in [10] explain that secure authentication protocols help preserve privacy of the users as they interact with their smart devices. Unfortunately, the resource-constrained nature of most of the smart devices renders it difficult to implement strong security protocols. In this regard, this paper makes the following contributions:

- A protocol that directly authenticates IoT devices is developed, devoid of the involvement of any central controller. This potentially solves the key escrow problems in majority of the current authentication protocols.
- Random nonces and pseudonyms are incorporated in the derivation of security tokens. This serves to preserve user anonymity and thwart any traceability attacks.
- The exchanged messages are enciphered through symmetric keys to protect them against eavesdropping and modifications. Effectively, this upholds both confidentiality and integrity of the communication process.
- Extensive security analysis is carried out to show the robustness of the proposed protocol against conventional IoT attack vectors.
- Comparative performance evaluation is executed to demonstrate that the developed protocol incurs the least computation and communication costs.

The rest of this paper is structured as follows: Sect. 2 gives a presentation of the related work while Sect. 3 discusses the employed system model. On the other hand, Sect. 4 presents the results obtained and discusses them. Towards the end of this paper, Sect. 5 gives the conclusions of this paper and offers some future research directions.

2 Related Work

The proliferation of attacks in IoT environment has seen numerous security protocols being developed to address these issues. Although majority of these schemes have fairly addressed security and privacy issues, majority of them have high computation and communication overheads [11, 12]. In addition, some security challenges still exist in majority of these protocols. For instance, the protocol in [13] has security issues as discussed by [14]. In addition, this scheme is vulnerable to Denial of Service (DoS) attacks and is unable to detect incorrect password login attempts. To curb these issues, lightweight and provably secure protocols have been introduced in [15] and [16]. To prevent black-hole attacks, trust-based and two-tier based protocols have been developed in [11] and [17] respectively. However, these two schemes solve privacy and authenticity issues at the expense of increased complexities. To boost security without compromising performance, Elliptic Curve Cryptography (ECC) based security approaches are presented in [18] and [19]. On the other hand, a blind anonymous authentication scheme is introduced in [20] too prevent eavesdropping attacks. However, since these three protocols are basically identity-based, they face key escrow challenges [21]. Although an efficient and secure scheme developed in [22] may address this problem, it inadvertently compromises user privacy during identity authentication. Therefore, a scheme in [23] has been developed to effectively deal with this challenge through biometrics based authentication.

De-synchronization attacks are other serious security issues that require immediate solution. For instance, although the protocol in [24] offers mutual authentication, it cannot withstand de-synchronization attacks. Therefore, the protocol in [25] has been designed to prevent these attacks. On the other hand, blockchain technology has also been deployed to offer security in IoT environment. For example, based on blockchain technology, a security preserving scheme is presented in [25]. Unfortunately, this technique has high complexity and communication overheads [26]. Similarly, the blockchain based privacy preserving protocol in [27] has high computation and communication overheads. On the other hand, the ECC and pseudonym based authentication protocol in [28] is lightweight and hence can address performance issues in both [27] and [29]. Similarly, the rating-based authentication protocol in [30] has lower computation costs and hence can address the performance issues in [27] and [29]. Using hash chains and blind signatures, an anonymous authentication scheme is developed in [31]. Although this scheme upholds sender privacy, it cannot trace malicious senders within the network. Similarly, a blind group signature based anonymous authentication protocol is presented in [32]. Although this scheme offers conditional anonymity, it incurs high communication and computation costs.

On its part, the protocol in [33] cannot withstand impersonation and key compromise attacks. In addition, it does not uphold user anonymity. Although the bilinear pairing based protocol in [34] offers mutual authentication, these pairing operations are time consuming [35]. Similarly, the scheme in [17] offers protection against black-hole attacks at the expense of very high complexity and communication costs. On the other hand, due to the centralized registration for secret cookie data creation, the scheme in [36] presents a single point of failure. To prevent exposure attacks, a key agreement protocol is introduced in [37]. However, a Physically Unclonable Functions (PUF) based scheme is introduced in [38] to thwart physical attacks. Unfortunately, PUFs challenge-response pairs are sometimes inconsistent and hence PUF based schemes have stability issues [39, 40]. According to [7], many privacy preserving protocols have been developed for IoT devices. However, most of these protocols have high computation complexities in addition to numerous security weaknesses.

3 System Model

The communicating entities involved in the proposed protocol include two IoT devices, which are labeled DV_1 and DV_2 as shown in Fig. 1.

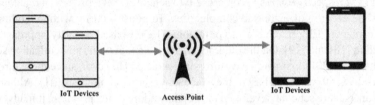

IoT Devices   Access Point   IoT Devices

Fig. 1. Network model

As shown in Fig. 1, the IoT devices in this network model communicate directly through a wireless access point. These devices have the same specifications and can therefore be regarded as peers. Table 1 presents the notations used in this protocol.

The three phases that characterize the proposed protocol include the handshake, authentication and the key agreement. The sub-sections below describes these phases in some greater details.

3.1 Handshake Phase

Before the two devices can start exchanging packets, they engage in a handshake in which they generate initial security tokens. This is a 3 step process as described below.

Step 1: DV1 stochastically generates its identity ID1 and some high entropy random nonce R1 which are then forwarded to DV2 in message {ID1, R1} over some secure channels.

Step 2: On receiving message {ID1, R1}, DV2 randomly generates its identity ID2 before deploying its master key MSK to generate cipher $C1 = EMSK((ID1 \oplus h(ID2 \| MSK)) \| (R1 \oplus ID1))$. Next, it derives its pseudo-identity $PID = h((ID1 \| ID2) \oplus MSK \oplus R1)$ which it stores in its memory. Lastly, it transmits {C1} to DV1 over secure channels.

Table 1. Notations

Notation	Description
R_i	Random number i
DV_1 & DV_2	Device 1 and device 2
MSK	DV_2 master key
E_k	Encipher using key k
ID_1 & ID_2	Unique identity of DV_1 & DV_2
PID	DV_2 pseudo-identity
D_k	Decipher using key k
SK	Symmetric key
S_{SK}	Session key
h (.)	One-way hashing function
‖	Concatenation operation
⊕	XOR operation

Step 3: After getting {C1} from DV2, DV1 stores parameter set {C1, ID1, R1} in its memory.

3.2 Authentication and Key Negotiation Phase

In this phase, the two devices utiize the security tokens obtained during the handshake phase to verify the authenticity of each other. This is accomplished in 7 steps that are elaborated below.

Step 1: Device DV_1 chooses high entropy random nonce R_2 before deriving security parameter $C_2 = R_2 \oplus h(ID_1 \| R_1)$. Next, DV_1 constructs message $M_1 = \{C_1, C_2\}$ and sends it over to DV_2 over public channels.

Step 2: Upon getting message M_1, DV_2 decrypts C_1 using its master key MSK by executing $D_1 = D_{MSK}(C_1)$ so as to obtain $ID_1^* \oplus h(ID_2^* \| MSK^*)$ and $R_1^* \oplus ID_1^*$. Next, it uses the decrypted message $ID_1^* \oplus h(ID_2^* \| MSK^*)$, its own identity ID_2 and master key MSK to compute device DV_1 identity, $ID_1^{New} = ID_1^* \oplus h(ID_2^* \| MSK^*) \oplus h(ID_2 \| MSK)$. Upon successful derivation of DV_1's identity, DV_2 proceeds to compute $R_1^{New} = R_1^* \oplus ID_1^* \oplus ID_1^{New}$. Finally, DV_2 computes $PID^* = h((ID_1^{New} \| ID_2) \oplus MSK \oplus R_1^{New})$. It then checks if $PID^* \overset{?}{=} PID$ such that the authentication request is rejected if the two values are not identical. Otherwise, DV_2 shifts to other subsequent steps.

Step 3: Using the received C_2 in message M_1, DV_2 computes $R_2^* = C_2 \oplus h(ID_1^{New} \| R_1^{New})$. This is followed by the updating of C_1 with C_1^* by substituting random nonce R_1^* with R_2^* in $C_1^* = E_{MSK}((ID_1^{New} \oplus h(ID_2 \| MSK)) \| (R_2^* \oplus ID_1^{New}))$.

Step 4: Device DV_2 chooses high entropy random nonce R_3 and derives a new symmetric key $SK = h(ID_1^{New} \oplus R_1^{New} \oplus R_2^*)$. Using the just computed encryption key, DV_2 generates authentication message $AM_1 = E_{SK}$

$((h((ID_1^{New} \oplus R_2^*)||R_1^{New}) \oplus R_3)||h(ID_1^{New}||R_1^{New}||R_2^*)||C_1^*)$. Lastly, DV_2 derive session key $S_{SK} = h(ID_1^{New}||R_1^{New}||R_2^*||R_3)$ that is sent in message $M_2 = \{S_{SK}\}$ over to device DV_1 using public channels.

Step 5: On receiving message M_2, device DV_1 deploys its identity ID_1 and high entropy random nonces R_1 and R_2 to derive symmetric key $SK^* = h(ID_1 \oplus R_1 \oplus R_2)$. It then utilizes this key to decrypt message AM_1 as $D_2 = D_{SK^*}(AM_1)$ to obtain $h((ID_1^{New^*} \oplus R_2^{New})||R_1^{New^*}) \oplus R_3^*)$, $h(ID_1^{New^*}||R_1^{New^*}||R_2^{New})$, and C_1^{New}. Next, DV_1 checks if the decrypted value $h(ID_1^{New^*}||R_1^{New^*}||R_2^{New})$ is equivalent to the computed value $h(ID_1||R_1||R_2)$. On condition that the two values are dissimilar, the authentication session is terminated. Otherwise, DV_1 computes $R_3^{New} = h((ID_1^{New^*} \oplus R_2^{New})||R_1^{New^*}) \oplus R_3^* \oplus h(ID_1 \oplus R_2)||R_1)$ that it uses to derive session key $S_{SK}^* = h(ID_1||R_1||R_2||R_3^{New})$. Lastly, DV_1 computes authentication message $AM_2 = h(S_{SK}^*||R_3^{New})$ that is then sent in $M_3 = \{AM_2\}$ to DV_2 over public channels as shown in Fig 2.

Step 6: After receiving message M_3 from DV_1, device DV_2 deploys session key S_{SK} and random nonce R_3 to check if $AM_2 \stackrel{?}{=} h(S_{SK}||R_3)$ such that the authentication session is terminated if this equation does not hold. Otherwise, it sets S_{SK} as the shared session key with devise DV_1.

Thereafter, it computes $PID^{New} = h((ID1^{New}||ID2) \oplus MSK \oplus R2)$ and substitutes PID with PID^{New} to be utilized during the next authentication phase. Finally, it composes acknowledgment message $AM3 = h((R2^* \oplus R3)||R1^{New})$ that is forwarded in $M4 = \{AM3\}$ to device $DV1$.

Step 7: Upon receiving message M_4, device DV_1 validates acknowledgment message AM_3 by confirming if $AM_3 \stackrel{?}{=} h((R_2 \oplus R_3^{New})||R_1)$.. Provided that these two values are equivalent, device DV_1 accepts session key S_{SK}^* and substitutes parameter set $\{R_1, C_1\}$ with $\{R_2, C_1^{New}\}$ in its memory. However, if AM_3 verification fails or device DV_1 fails to get this acknowledgment message within the stipulated time, the session is terminated. Essentially, this implies that device DV_1 commences a fresh session.

4   Results and Discussion

In this section, the proposed protocol is evaluated using security and performance metrics. To accomplish security analysis, different lemmas are formulated and proofed. On the other hand, performance evaluation is accomplished using computation and communication complexities.

4.1 Security Analysis

In this section, it is shown that the proposed protocol offers untraceability and anonymity. In addition, it resists attacks such as de-synchronization and known secret key leakage attacks.

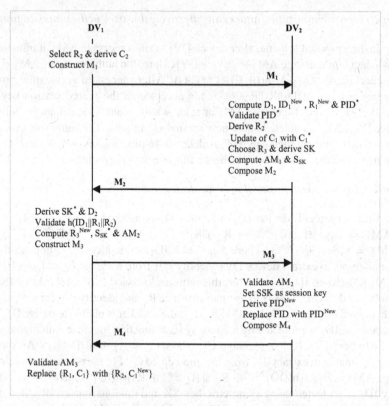

Fig. 2. Authentication and Key Negotiation

Lemma 1: The proposed protocol offers device untraceability.

Proof: In this protocol, an attacker is unable to track the origin of the exchanged messages. This is achieved by employing transcient security parameters during the authentication and key negotiation phase. For instance, during the authentication process, messages $M_1 = \{C_1, C_2\}$, $\{AM_1, AM_2\}$, and AM_3 are transient in nature. Here, $C_1 = E_{MSK}((ID_1 \oplus h(ID_2\|MSK))\|(R_1 \oplus ID_1))$, $C_2 = R_2 \oplus h(ID_1\|R_1)$, $AM_1 = E_{SK} ((h((ID_1^{New} \oplus R_2^*)\|R_1^{New}) \oplus R_3)\|h(ID_1^{New}\|R_1^{New}\|R_2^*)\|C_1^*)$, $AM_2 = h(S_{SK}^*\|R_3^{New})$, and $AM_3 = h((R_2^* \oplus R_3)\|R_1^{New})$. Evidently, all these parameters incorporate high entropy random nonce R_i which are stochastically generated at the devices. Consequently, all the exchanged messages are session-specific. In addition, towards the end of each authentication and key negotiation phase, parameter set $\{R_1, C_1\}$ are replaced with refreshed values $\{R_2, C_1^{New}\}$. Suppose that an adversary captures authentication messages belonging to either device DV_1 or device DV_2. In the proposed protocol, the intercepted messages cannot permit the attacker to distinguish whether two sessions belong to the same device and hence tracking a particular device is infeasible.

Lemma 2: De-synchronization attacks are effectively thwarted in the proposed protocol.

Proof: In the proposed scheme, after device DV_2 verifies message AM_2, it transmits an acknowledgement message AM_3 to device DV_1. Here, the authenticity of AM_3 is verified by checking if $AM_3 \overset{?}{=} h((R_2 \oplus R_3^{New})\|R_1)$.. After successful verification process, session key $S_{SK}^* = h(ID_1\|R_1\|R_2\|R_3^{New})$ is accepted as the shared session key with device DV_2. However, if message AM_2 or acknowledgement AM_3 cannot be delivered to device DV_1, S_{SK}^* is deleted and a new session is initiated. The same will take place when acknowledgement message AM_3 is delayed. In this new session, device DV_1 and DV_2 re-negotiate the session key and hence this attack is prevented.

Lemma 3:   The proposed protocol upholds device anonymity.

Proof: In this protocol, device DV_1 identity ID_1 is masked in message $M_1 = \{C_1, C_2\}$, $AM_1 = E_{SK}((h((ID_1^{New} \oplus R_2^*)\|R_1^{New}) \oplus R_3)\|h(ID_1^{New}\|R_1^{New}\|R_2^*)\|C_1^*)$ and $AM_2 = h(S_{SK}^*\|R_3^{New})$, where $S_{SK}^* = h(ID_1\|R_1\|R_2\|R_3^{New})$. Suppose that an attacker attempts to extract device DV_1 identity ID_1 from message $C_1 = E_{MSK}((ID_1 \oplus h(ID_2\|MSK))\|(R_1 \oplus ID_1))$. However, this requires knowledge of master key MSK for device DV_2 to decrypt C_1, as well as random nonce R_1 and identity ID_2 for device DV_2. As such, devoid of $\{MSK, ID_2\}$ or $\{MSK, R_1\}$, the attacker is unable to derive ID_1 from C_1. In addition, ID_1 is protected by a one-way hash function together with high entropy random numbers $\{R_1, R_2\}$ in message C_2, where $C_2 = R_2 \oplus h(ID_1\|R_1)$. As such, an adversary is unable to extract ID_1 from the intercepted C_2. For the case of authentication message $AM_1 = E_{SK}((h((ID_1^{New} \oplus R_2^*)\|R_1^{New}) \oplus R_3)\|h(ID_1^{New}\|R_1^{New}\|R_2^*)\|C_1^*)$, identity ID_1 is protected using symmetric key SK and random nonces $\{R_1, R_2\}$. Once again, an attacker is unable to extract ID_1 from AM_1. Similarly, ID_1 is protected using one-way hash function together with random nonces $\{R_1, R_2, R_3\}$ in message AM_2 $= h(S_{SK}^*\|R_3^{New})$, where $S_{SK}^* = h(ID_1\|R_1\|R_2\|R_3^{New})$. Consequently, the proposed protocol offers anonymity during the authentication and key negotiation phase.

Lemma 4:   Known secret key leakage attacks are thwarted in this protocol.

Proof: During the authentication and key negotiattion process, session key S_{SK} is derived, where $S_{SK} = h(ID_1^{New}\|R_1^{New}\|R_2^*\|R_3)$. This session key incorporates device DV_1 identity ID_1 and three random nonces $\{R_1, R_2, R_3\}$ protected via one-way hashing operation. Here, R_1 and R_2 are generated by device DV_1 in different scenarios, while random nonce R_3 is generated at device DV_2. This random and independent generation of random nonces $\{R_1, R_2, R_3\}$ implies that the derived session key is unique for each authentication instant. As such, an adversary cannot compute the session key for subsequent authentication session using the captured current session key.

Lemma 5: The proposed protocol offers protection against eavesdropping attacks.

Proof: Suppose that an attacker wants to intercept secret parameters such as master key MSK and device real identities ID_1 and ID_2. To achieve this, messages $M_1 = \{C_1, C_2\}$, $M_2 = \{S_{SK}\}$, $M_3 = \{AM_2\}$ and $M_4 = \{AM_3\}$ must be captured. Here, $C_1 = E_{MSK}((ID_1 \oplus h(ID_2\|MSK))\|(R_1 \oplus ID_1))$, $C_2 = R_2 \oplus h(ID_1\|R_1)$, $S_{SK} = h(ID_1^{New}\|R_1^{New}\|R_2^*\|R_3)$,

$AM_2 = h(S_{SK}{}^* \| R_3{}^{New})$ and $AM_3 = h((R_2{}^* \oplus R_3) \| R_1{}^{New})$. However, identity ID_1 is encrypted in C_1 and hashed in both C_2 and S_{SK}. On the other hand, identity ID_2 is hashed and enciphered in C_1. Similarly, master key MSK is hashed and encrypted in C_1. Since it is computationally infeasible to reverse the one-way hash function, and an attacker has no access to the secret master key, the decryption of security parameter C_1 is infeasible and hence eavesdropping attack flops.

Lemma 6: Forgery attacks are prevented in the proposed protocol.

Proof: The assumption made here is that an attacker wants to fool both devices DV_1 and DV_2 through message fabrication. To achieve this, bogus messages $C_1 = E_{MSK}((ID_1 \oplus h(ID_2 \| MSK)) \| (R_1 \oplus ID_1))$, $AM_1 = E_{SK}((h(((ID_1{}^{New} \oplus R_2{}^*) \| R_1{}^{New}) \oplus R_3) \| h(ID_1{}^{New} \| R_1{}^{New} \| R_2{}^*) \| C_1{}^*)$, $C_2 = R_2 \oplus h(ID_1 \| R_1)$, $AM_2 = h(S_{SK}{}^* \| R_3{}^{New})$ and $AM_3 = h((R_2{}^* \oplus R_3) \| R_1{}^{New})$ need to be constructed. However, the construction of these messages require encryption key SK and master key MSK. In addition, the attacker needs to determine the hashing function deployed for the construction of these messages. However, since all these parameters are unavailable to the adversary, this attack fails.

Lemma 7:   The proposed protocol offers perfect forward key secrecy.

Proof: Suppose that an attacker is interested in deriving the session key $S_{SK}{}^{New}$ for the subsequent authentication session. To accomplish this, message M_2 is intercepted, where $M_2 = \{S_{SK}\}$. Here, session key $S_{SK} = h(ID_1{}^{New} \| R_1{}^{New} \| R_2{}^* \| R_3)$. Evidently, this requires correct generation of random nonces $R_1{}^{New}$, $R_2{}^*$ and R_3, as well as device DV_1 identity $ID_1{}^{New}$. Since these three nonces are randomly generated, it is infeasible to accurately generate all of them. In addition, by Lemma 5, an adversary cannot determine device identities ID_1 and ID_2. As such, perfect key secrecy is upheld.

4.2   Performance Evaluation

In this sub-section, the computation overheads, communication costs and functionality of the proposed protocol are presented. Thereafter, comparisons are also made with other related schemes so as to provide the basis for the appraisal of the proposed protocol.

Computation Costs: A typical authentication and key negotiation phase involves operations such as one-way hashing (T_H), symmetric encryption (T_{SE}), ECC point multiplication (T_M), symmetric decryption (T_{SD}) and ECC point addition (T_A). In the proposed protocol, $7T_H$ and $1T_{SD}$ operations are executed on device DV_1 while $9T_H$, $1T_{SD}$ and $2T_{SE}$ operations are carried out on device DV_2. As such, the total computation cost in this scheme is $16T_H$, $2T_{SD}$ and $2T_{SE}$. Based on the values in [41], single T_H, T_{SE} / T_{SD}, T_M and T_A execution times are 0.0023 ms, 0.0046 ms, 2.226 ms and 0.0288 ms respectively. As such, the total computation cost of the proposed protocol is 0.0552 ms as shown in Table 2.

Table 2. Computation costs

Scheme	Costs (ms)
[16]	0.8
[24]	0.88
[25]	0.64
[33]	8.98
Proposed	0.0552

It is evident from Table 2 that the scheme in [33] incurs the highest computation costs followed by the protocols in [16, 24] and [25] respectively. On the other hand, the proposed protocol has the lowest computation overheads. Owing to the processing limitations of D2D devices, the proposed protocol is the most ideal for these devices.

Communication Costs: Communication Costs: During the authentication and key agreement process, messages M_1, M_2, M_3 and M_4 are exchanged between DV_1 and DV_2. Here, $M_1 = \{C_1, C_2\}$, $M_2 = \{S_{SK}\}$, $M_3 = \{AM_2\}$, $M_4 = \{AM_3\}$, $C_1 = E_{MSK}((ID_1 \oplus h(ID_2\|MSK))\|(R_1 \oplus ID_1))$, $C_2 = R_2 \oplus h(ID_1\|R_1)$, $S_{SK} = h(ID_1{}^{New}\|R_1{}^{New}\|R_2{}^*\|R_3)$, $AM_2 = h(S_{SK}{}^*\|R_3{}^{New})$ and $AM_3 = h((R_2{}^* \oplus R_3)\|R_1{}^{New})$. Using the values in [41], the output sizes of hash function (SHA-1), timestamps, identity, symmetric encryption / decryption and ECC point are 160 bits, 32 bits, 160 bits, 128 bits and 160 bits respectively. As such, $C_1 = 128$ bits, $C_2 = 160$ bits; and hence M_1 is 288 bits long. On the other hand, $S_{SK} = AM_2 = AM_3 = 160$ bits; therefore $M_2 = M_3 = M_4 = 160$ bits in length. Consequently, the total communication cost of the proposed protocol is 768 bits as shown in Table 3.

Table 3. Communication costs

Scheme	Costs (bits)
[16]	2624
[24]	2640
[25]	2856
[33]	2016
Proposed	768

As shown in Fig. 3, the scheme in [25] has the highest communication costs followed by the schemes in [16, 24] and [33] respectively. On the other hand, the proposed protocol has the least communication cost of only 768 bits.

Since most of the D2D devices are limited in terms of battery power and communication abilities, the proposed protocol places the least constrain on these devices. As such, it is the most suitable for deployment in this environment.

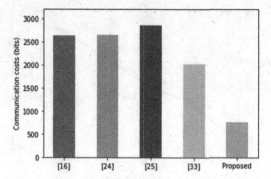

Fig. 3. Communication costs comparisons

To investigate the effect of device density on the computation costs and end-to-end latencies, a computer runing on Windows 10 Pro 64-bit with 2.4 GHz Intel Core i5-4210U CPU and 4 GB of RAM is deployed to implement the proposed protocol. Java pairing based cryptography and Bouncy Castle cryptographic libraries are used. Figure 4 shows the variation of communication costs as a function of the number of IoT devices and number of messages sent.

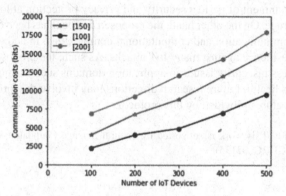

Fig. 4. Communication costs variations

As shown in Fig. 4, for a given number of IoT devices, the higher the messages transmitted the higher the communication costs and vice versa. In general, as the number of IoT devices increases so does the communication costs. Figure 5 shows the variations of end to end latencies as a function of the number of messages exchanged.

It is evident from Fig. 5 that as the number of messages increases, the values of end to end latencies increase. This is attributed to the increased processing that has to be executed at the IoT devices when the numbers of messages increase.

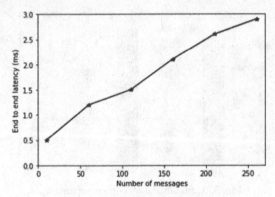

Fig. 5. End to end latency variations

5 Conclusion and Future Work

The IoT communication has found applications in a number of application domains to offer convenience and efficiency to the users. However, there are many efficiency, security and performance issues that remain unresolved in this communication environment. To this end, many security protocols have been developed in an effort to address these issues. However, the attainment of perfect security and privacy protection at low complexities still remain a mirage. On the other hand, the proposed protocol has been demonstrated to have the least communication and computational complexities. In addition, it has been shown to have resilience against many IoT attacks. As such, the proposed protocol can potentially address insecurity issues in application domains such as smart cities, smart homes and smart health. Future research directions may involve the formal verification of the security features provided by this protocol.

Acknowledgement. This work is supported by Natural Science Foundation of Top Talent of SZTU (grant No. GDRC202135).

References

1. Hao, Y., Helo, P.: The role of wearable devices in meeting the needs of cloud manufacturing: a case study. Robot. Comput.-Integr. Manuf. **45**, 168–179 (2017)
2. Dang, T.K., Pham, C.D., Nguyen, T.L.: A pragmatic elliptic curve cryptography-based extension for energy-efficient device-to-device communications in smart cities. Sustain. Cities Soc. **56**, 102097 (2020)
3. Habibzadeh, H., Nussbaum, B.H., Anjomshoa, F., Kantarci, B., Soyata, T.: A survey on cybersecurity, data privacy, and policy issues in cyber-physical system deployments in smart cities. Sustain. Cities Soc. **50**, 101660 (2019)
4. Dang, T.K., Tran, K.T.: The meeting of acquaintances: a cost-efficient authentication scheme for light-weight objects with transient trust level and plurality approach. Secur. Commun. Net. **2019**(8123259), 1–18 (2019)

5. Zhang, Y., Cheng, K., Khan, F., Alturki, R., Khan, R., Rehman, A.U.: A mutual authentication scheme for establishing secure device-to-device communication sessions in the edge-enabled smart cities. J. Inf. Secur. Appl. **58**, 102683 (2021)
6. Nyangaresi, V.O., Morsy, M.A.: Towards privacy preservation in internet of drones. In: 2021 IEEE 6th International Forum on Research and Technology for Society and Industry (RTSI), 306–311. IEEE (2021)
7. Li, J., Zhang, W., Dabra, V., Choo, K.K.R., Kumari, S., Hogrefe, D.: AEP-PPA: an anonymous, efficient and provably-secure privacy-preserving authentication protocol for mobile services in smart cities. J. Netw. Comput. Appl. **134**, 52–61 (2019)
8. Xia, X., Ji, S., Vijayakumar, P., Shen, J., Rodrigues, J.J.: An efficient anonymous authentication and key agreement scheme with privacy-preserving for smart cities. Int. J. Distrib. Sens. Netw. **17**(6), 15501477211026804 (2021)
9. Nyangaresi, V.O.: Hardware assisted protocol for attacks prevention in ad hoc networks. In: Miraz, M.H., Southall, G., Ali, M., Ware, A., Soomro, S. (eds.) iCETiC 2021. LNICSSITE, vol. 395, pp. 3–20. Springer, Cham (2021). https://doi.org/10.1007/978-3-030-90016-8_1
10. Malik, M.N., Azam, M.A., Ehatisham-Ul-Haq, M., Ejaz, W., Khalid, A.: ADLAuth: passive authentication based on activity of daily living using heterogeneous sensing in smart cities. Sensors **19**(11), 2466 (2019)
11. Yaseen, Q.M., Aldwairi, M.: An enhanced AODV protocol for avoiding black holes in MANET. Procedia Comput. Sci. **134**, 371–376 (2018)
12. Shen, J., Chang, S., Shen, J., Liu, Q., Sun, X.: A lightweight multi-layer authentication protocol for wireless body area networks. Futur. Gener. Comput. Syst. **78**, 956–963 (2018)
13. Gope, P., Hwang, T.: An efficient mutual authentication and key agreement scheme preserving strong anonymity of the mobile user in global mobility networks. J. Netw. Comput. Appl. **62**, 1–8 (2016)
14. Li, X., Peng, J., Niu, J., Wu, F., Liao, J., Choo, K.K.R.: A robust and energy efficient authentication protocol for industrial internet of things. IEEE Internet Things J. **5**(3), 1606–1615 (2017)
15. Khemissa, H., Tandjaoui, D., Bouzefrane, S.: An ultra-lightweight authentication scheme for heterogeneous wireless sensor networks in the context of internet of things. In: Bouzefrane, S., Banerjee, S., Sailhan, F., Boumerdassi, S., Renault, E. (eds.) MSPN 2017. LNCS, vol. 10566, pp. 49–62. Springer, Cham (2017). https://doi.org/10.1007/978-3-319-67807-8_4
16. Alzahrani, B.A., Irshad, A., Albeshri, A., Alsubhi, K.: A provably secure and lightweight patient-healthcare authentication protocol in wireless body area networks. Wireless Pers. Commun. **117**(1), 47–69 (2021). https://doi.org/10.1007/s11277-020-07237-x
17. Yasin, A., Abu, Z.M.: Detecting and isolating black-hole attacks in MANET using timer based baited technique. Wirel. Commun. Mob. Comput. **2018**, 1–10 (2018)
18. Chaudhry, S.A., Naqvi, H., Sher, M., Farash, M.S., Hassan, M.U.: An improved and provably secure privacy preserving authentication protocol for SIP. Peer-to-Peer Netw. Appl. **10**(1), 1–15 (2015). https://doi.org/10.1007/s12083-015-0400-9
19. Zhong, H., Huang, B., Cui, J., Xu, Y., Liu, L.: Conditional privacy-preserving authentication using registration list in vehicular ad hoc networks. IEEE Access **6**, 2241–2250 (2018)
20. Vasco, M., Pozo, A., Soriente, C.: A key for John Doe: modeling and designing anonymous password authenticated key exchange protocols. IEEE Trans. Dependable Secure Comput. **18**(3), 1336–1353 (2021)
21. Nyangaresi, V.O.: Provably secure protocol for 5G HetNets. In: 2021 IEEE International Conference on Microwaves, Antennas, Communications and Electronic Systems (COMCAS), 17–22. IEEE (2021)
22. Wei, J., Phuong, T., Yang, G.: An efficient privacy preserving message authentication scheme for internet of-things. IEEE Trans. Industr. Inf. **17**(1), 617–626 (2021)

23. Blasco, J., Peris-Lopez, P.: On the feasibility of low-cost wearable sensors for multi-modal biometric verification. Sensors **18**(9), 2782 (2018)
24. Ibrahim, M.H., Kumari, S., Das, A.K., Wazid, M., Odelu, V.: Secure anonymous mutual authentication for star two-tier wireless body area networks. Comput. Methods Programs Biomed. **135**, 37–50 (2016)
25. Li, X., Ibrahim, M.H., Kumari, S., Sangaiah, A.K., Gupta, V., Choo, K.K.R.: Anonymous mutual authentication and key agreement scheme for wearable sensors in wireless body area networks. Comput. Netw. **129**, 429–443 (2017)
26. Nyangaresi, V.O., Abduljabbar, Z.A., Al Sibahee, M.A., Abduljaleel, I.Q., Abood, E.W.: Towards security and privacy preservation in 5G networks. In: 2021 29th Telecommunications Forum (TELFOR), pp. 1–4. IEEE (2021)
27. Shen, M., Tang, X., Zhu, L., Du, X., Guizani, M.: Privacy-preserving support vector machine training over blockchain-based encrypted IoT data in smart cities. IEEE Internet Things J. **6**(5), 7702–7712 (2019)
28. Reddy, A.G., Suresh, D., Phaneendra, K., Shin, J.S., Odelu, V.: Provably secure pseudo-identity based device authentication for smart cities environment. Sustain. Cities Soc. **41**, 878–885 (2018)
29. Singh, P., Nayyar, A., Kaur, A., Ghosh, U.: Blockchain and fog based architecture for internet of everything in smart cities. Future Internet **12**(4), 61 (2020)
30. Tran, K.K., Pham, M.K., Dang, T.K.: A light-weight tightening authentication scheme for the objects' encounters in the meetings. In: Dang, Tran Khanh, Küng, Josef, Wagner, Roland, Thoai, Nam, Takizawa, Makoto (eds.) FDSE 2018. LNCS, vol. 11251, pp. 83–102. Springer, Cham (2018). https://doi.org/10.1007/978-3-030-03192-3_8
31. Dimitriou, T., Karame, G.O.: Enabling anonymous authorization and rewarding in the smart grid. IEEE Trans. Dependable Secure Comput. **14**(5), 565–572 (2017)
32. Kong, W., Shen, J., Vijayakumar, P., Cho, Y., Chang, V.: A practical group blind signature scheme for privacy protection in smart grid. J. Parallel Distrib. Comput. **136**, 29–39 (2020)
33. Mandal, S., Mohanty, S., Majhi, B.: Cryptanalysis and enhancement of an anonymous self-certified key exchange protocol. Wireless Pers. Commun. **99**(2), 863–891 (2017). https://doi.org/10.1007/s11277-017-5156-5
34. He, D., Kumar, N., Khan, M.K., Wang, L., Shen, J.: Efficient privacy-aware authentication scheme for mobile cloud computing services. IEEE Syst. J. **12**(2), 1621–1631 (2018)
35. Nyangaresi, V.O., et al.: Provably secure session key agreement protocol for unmanned aerial vehicles packet exchanges. In: 2021 International Conference on Electrical, Computer and Energy Technologies (ICECET), pp. 1–6. IEEE (2021)
36. Wang, K.H., Chen, C.M., Fang, W., Wu, T.Y.: A secure authentication scheme for internet of things. Pervasive Mob. Comput. **42**, 15–26 (2017)
37. Wu, L., Wang, J., Choo, K.K.R., He, D.: Secure key agreement and key protection for mobile device user authentication. IEEE Trans. Inf. Forensics Secur. **14**(2), 319–330 (2019)
38. Boyapally, H., et al.: Safe is the new smart: PUF-based authentication for load modification-resistant smart meters. IEEE Trans. Dependable Secure Comput. **19**(1), 663–680 (2022)
39. Suzuki, M., Ueno, R., Homma, N., Aoki, T.: Efficient fuzzy extractors based on ternary debiasing method for biased physically unclonable functions. IEEE Trans. Circ. Syst. **66**(2), 616–629 (2019)
40. Nyangaresi, V.O., Petrovic, N.: Efficient PUF based authentication protocol for internet of drones. In: 2021 International Telecommunications Conference (ITC-Egypt), pp. 1–4. IEEE (2021)
41. Alzahrani, B.A., Chaudhry, S.A., Barnawi, A., Al-Barakati, A., Shon, T.: An anonymous device to device authentication protocol using ECC and self certified public keys usable in Internet of Things based autonomous devices. Electronics **9**(3), 520 (2020)

Evaluating CoAP, OSCORE, DTLS and HTTPS for Secure Device Communication

Kristofer Nedergaard, Bhupjit Singh(✉), and Birger Andersen

DTU Engineering Technology, Technical University of Denmark,
2750 Ballerup, Denmark
KNE@ICEpower.dk, {bhsi,birad}@dtu.dk
https://www.dtu.dk

Abstract. The purpose of this paper is to explore the differences and relations between the protocols CoAP, OSCORE, DTLS and HTTPS. Our focus is at performance and the general security benefits of the different protocols. We evaluate the feasibility of using CoAP encrypted with OSCORE or DTLS as opposed to using HTTPS/1.1 or HTTPS/3. We find the CoAP based solutions to be more performant than HTTPS, however we also find them to be harder to implement, less widespread and potentially more insecure than HTTPS. From these findings, in most scenarios we recommend implementing solutions based on HTTPS if the performance and overhead can be tolerated.

Keywords: CoAP · OSCORE · DTLS · HTTPS · Secure communication

1 Introduction

During the past decade, we have been experiencing a significant uplift in small home appliances and sensor stations that are connected to the internet. As our homes become increasingly more connected, we are sharing larger parts of our lives on the internet. This exposes us to potential intruders that can remotely monitor our daily lives.

A range of different methods to secure data transfer from our homes to cloud or from Device to Device (D2D) has arrived, some of which are targeted specifically toward devices. One of the most popular such protocols has become CoAP (Constrained Application Protocol) [1], and more specifically, CoAP secured by DTLS (Datagram Transport Layer Security) [2]. Many cloud providers, however, do not receive data directly in the form of CoAP/DTLS. Instead they receive data primarily through protocols that are traditionally implemented for unconstrained network environments like HTTPS (Hypertext Transport Protocol) [3]. This presents a problem that has been solved by implementing intermediate proxies that translate between CoAP/DTLS and HTTPS/TLS. This proxying however, inherently introduces a security risk at each proxying point, as the DTLS data will need to be decrypted and re-encrypted for further transport as TLS [4].

© ICST Institute for Computer Sciences, Social Informatics and Telecommunications Engineering 2023
Published by Springer Nature Switzerland AG 2023. All Rights Reserved
T. Pereira et al. (Eds.): IoECon 2022, LNICST 458, pp. 117–132, 2023.
https://doi.org/10.1007/978-3-031-25222-8_10

In this paper we explore two different ways to circumvent the security issue with proxying data between different protocols. The first is to encrypt the entirety of the message separately from the transport protocol, something the protocol of OSCORE aims to accomplish [5]. The second is to explore the feasibility of using HTTPS directly on the device, which effectively eliminates the need for proxying between protocols altogether. We also provide an overview of different protocols and their performance and security advantages and disadvantages.

In Sect. 2 we introduce necessary background knowledge about the different protocols. Section 3 and 4 present a test setup and the results of the tests. In Sect. 5 and 6, the results are interpreted and the implementations of protocols are discussed. Following this we present a more in-depth review of the security of the protocols in Sect. 7. Sections 8 and 9 discuss and conclude on our findings.

2   Background

Computers and networking become more and more advanced and we find ways to make our computers smaller, both in terms of physical size and power consumption. This has allowed for devices that we embed into items/everything that we use in our daily lives. Things that are today ranging from light bulbs to kitchen appliances. We often like these devices to be controllable and report back to us remotely, perhaps even when we are not at home, but often, we would also like to keep our data private and secure.

In this section we give an overview of some of the protocols in use today and give some insight about them in a historical aspect that will shed some light on why the networking protocols explored in this paper exist and explain each of their different original purposes.

2.1   HTTP and HTTPS

HTTP, the Hypertext Transport Protocol was introduced in 1996 [6]. HTTP has evolved to become one of the most widespread networked application protocols in existence. It has been, and still is being used for many websites. Because of its widespread use, it is also being used in many IoT device projects, even if it may not be the fastest or most secure option. HTTP is inherently insecure and messages are transferred in plaintext. This allows for anyone with networking skills to pick up and read transferred messages by sniffing tools containing sensitive data like passwords, credit card information, or perhaps just what temperature your home has at a given time. No matter what kind of information, it definitely presents a security risk. HTTPS (Hypertext Transport Protocol Secure) was introduced to mitigate security issues of the HTTP protocol was introduced [7].

HTTPS extends HTTP and adds TLS encryption in order to secure the connection between a server and a client. HTTPS and TLS were originally designed for use over the reliable TCP transport protocol which is what the original HTTP protocol was based on, but in recent times, an effort has been made towards switching from TCP to the unreliable lightweight UDP transport protocol in order to circumvent the overhead in TCP and speed up communication over HTTPS. This effort is what has evolved into QUIC [8] - a protocol which allows HTTPS and TLS connections over UDP, effectively replacing TCP in order to gain a performance increase. Along with QUIC, a new standard for HTTP was defined: HTTP/3.

2.2   CoAP and DTLS

A challenge has always been how to proceed in regard to transferring collected data to and from each device and send them to a cloud server. This, however, has presented itself to be an issue in IoT devices because of adverse network conditions and the fact that many devices are battery operated. This constrained environment has lead to a need for a new networking protocol to break with traditional TCP-based protocols that expect close to perfect networking conditions. This is why CoAP, the Constrained Application Protocol was introduced [9].

CoAP has been designed to mimic the REST capabilities of a normal HTTP server, but due to the aforementioned constrained environments, it has been designed to transfer data over UDP instead of TCP. Furthermore CoAP significantly reduces the header size and as opposed to HTTP, the header's size is also not of variable size which allows for more precise calculations and dependable transfers. CoAP is also significantly better at handling scenarios with high amounts of packet loss. CoAP implements a publisher/subscriber system like the MQTT (Message Queue Telemetry Transport) protocol, where it is possible to subscribe to data through a broker instead of asking the other device. This gives the possibility of receiving data from one another without being able to connect directly, but instead only contacting a common data broker [10].

Securing the CoAP connection is by definition in the RFC (Request for Comments), done via Datagram Transport Layer Security, DTLS [11]. DTLS is based on TLS as in HTTPS. It therefore also provides the same security. DTLS, while designed to be very similar to TLS, provides additional functionality to handle the unreliability of UDP. This also means that DTLS can function well even in tough network conditions with many packet losses. DTLS allows for a secure end-to-end connection between two devices when communicating via CoAP over UDP in a very similar manner to what is seen with TLS and HTTP. Transferring secure data over CoAP has for a while been synonymous with using DTLS.

2.3   OSCORE

OSCORE can be seen as an extension to CoAP. It alters the options processing of CoAP and therefore also modifies the original definition of CoAP. Due to this, changes to CoAP implementation are required to have a fully functional OSCORE implementation. OSCORE is defined in a way that allows it to be transferred over CoAP as well as HTTP. OSCORE also does not encrypt the CoAP messaging and token layer, so when transferring OSCORE encrypted data, these layers will still be in plaintext [12].

This means that OSCORE, while slightly changing the specifications of CoAP, is designed in a way that can be implemented across multiple different networking protocols.

OSCORE was designed specifically to mitigate an issue that presents itself when using CoAP with DTLS. This issue is that, in order to connect to a cloud solution or any other kind of HTTP server, it is often necessary to introduce a intermediate proxy that translates between CoAP and HTTP [13]. The same is the case the other way around, when a HTTP client has to connect to a CoAP server. OSCORE aims to improve this situation by encrypting the payload itself, somewhat independently of the protocol that transports the CoAP encrypted data. By doing this, OSCORE improves upon one of the bigger security concerns of CoAP with DTLS, completely eliminating the potential risks associated with CoAP↔HTTP proxying. Figure 1 further visualizes this.

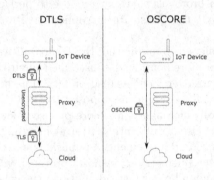

Fig. 1. A visual representation of the differences between proxying DTLS and OSCORE.

OSCORE currently does not define a method of key exchange. This can be seen as an advantage in that the key exchange protocol can be chosen independently of OSCORE. This, however, also has a side effect as different implementations of OSCORE might not be compatible if the key exchange algorithms differ. Because of the design of OSCORE, it can even be possible to encrypt the CoAP messages with DTLS and OSCORE alongside each other, as well as encrypting with DTLS or TLS in only parts of the journey between proxies and endpoints.

2.4   Comparison of Protocols

Figure 2 shows the different layers that protocols are working on. This shows the reason why OSCORE encryption can persist through proxies, but TLS and DTLS cannot. QUIC implements TLS functionality as part of the QUIC protocol, so it can be seen as delivering the same kind of functionality as TLS on its own. Each protocol has a number of advantages and disadvantages.

In Table 1 some of these are shown. While HTTPS initially was a TCP-only protocol, more recent editions have been extended to work with UDP. This eliminates some overhead and makes it better suited for device communication.

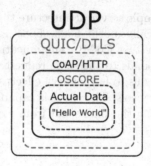

Fig. 2. Slightly simplified visual overview of the layering of different protocols.

Table 1. A comparison between different network protocols.

	Transport	Proxy safe	Forward secrecy	Header size
HTTPS/1	TCP	No	Yes	Variable
HTTPS/3	UDP	No	Yes	Variable
DTLS	UDP	No	Yes	11 bytes
OSCORE	UDP	Yes	No	11 bytes

One issue with this might be that it requires the server to support HTTPS over QUIC, which can be troublesome as HTTPS/3 is not in widespread use yet. CoAP has always been UDP-only, which ensures that the transport overhead stays reasonable low.

3   Test Setup of Protocols

In order to perform a fair test, we have generated a set of random bytes in a few different sizes, ranging from 25 bytes to 2500 bytes as sample data to be used across the protocols and test environments. For performance measurements the application will attempt to transfer the data 10000 times and compute the average time for completion. In all timing measurements these average times are the reported values.

3.1   OSCORE and DTLS

As both OSCORE and DTLS is generally transported via the CoAP protocol, it made sense to find a CoAP library capable of handling both of these. In these tests, the Californium Library by Eclipse Foundation was chosen for this specific purpose [14]. The Californium library has lightweight sample implementation of communication with both CoAP/DTLS and CoAP/OSCORE. Californium also includes examples for handling unencrypted CoAP communication so it is possible to compare the different protocol overheads against using plain text directly.

The tests consist of a simple server architecture that can respond to requests on multiple ports, specifically ports 5683, 5684 and 5685 for respectively OSCORE, DTLS and Plain Text CoAP communication. Regardless of the protocol in use, the server responds to the same request URL with the same data. Californium therefore allows us to have a very effective comparison between the different CoAP security protocols. The client is capable of requesting a resource from the server and recording the time spent from request to response.

3.2 HTTPS/3

Unfortunately, Californium Library only supports CoAP communication. Because of that, the HTTPS/3.0 test setup looks different to the CoAP based protocols. However, we have tried to keep the structure very similar. The exact same naming scheme for retrieving the same bytes has been kept, the client is entirely implemented in Java alongside the CoAP client, and the actual data transferred between the server and client is identical to the CoAP test setup.

The HTTPS/3.0 server is set up with a Caddy2 server [15]. This is capable of answering over TCP and also QUIC which is needed in this test setup. It means that both HTTP/1.1 and HTTP/3 can to be tested and compared on the same server setup. The Caddy2 server specifically has an opt-in functionality 'experimental_http3' that needs to be enabled for allowing Caddy2 to respond via QUIC over UDP. As this is a local test without a proper domain name, the local Caddy2 root certificate also needs to be installed in the test client machine's trust store. Caddy2 serves a QUIC through the QUIC-Go library [16]. This is a common Go library seen in a few recent, but well-known, web-application projects like Caddy, Traefik and SyncThing.

For the client set up, the flupke HTTPS/3 library has been chosen [17]. This library is capable of connecting to secured HTTPS/3 websites and retrieving data in a very similar fashion to the Californium CoAP library. It extends the default HttpClient implementation in Java and because of this it is very easy to implement a HTTP/3 Client with flupke.

3.3 HTTPS/1.1

For good measurement, a test setup with HTTP/1.1 is also prepared. With this we can test whether there is an increase or decrease in performance between HTTPS/3 over QUIC and HTTPS/1.1 over TCP. The HTTPS/1.1 test setup is almost entirely identical to the HTTPS/3. Caddy2 supports answering in both HTTPS/1.1 and HTTPS/3, so no configuration changes are needed.

On the client side, the flupke library for HTTP/3 extends the default Http-Client in Java. This means that the only difference between the test setup for HTTPS/3 and HTTPS/1.1 will be to instantiate the HTTP/1.1 client from the built-in java libraries.

3.4 Test Machine

The tests were performed using two identical VirtualBox Virtual Machines with 1 GB of RAM and a single processor core at 100% capacity allotted. The virtual machines were running Ubuntu 20.04.3 LTS. The host machine was a 6-core, 12-thread Intel I5-11400 with 32 GB of physical memory, running Ubuntu 20.04 LTS. The virtual machines were connected with a VirtualBox Internal Network without outside interference. The Californium library does not build as a whole out of the box from their git repository. Because of this, each virtual machine is installed with a full desktop environment along with a Java IDE. This allows for running the small subset of classes that we need from Californium. In the internal network between the virtual machines, a larger MTU (Maximum Transfer Unit) than what is normally present in networking is allowed. This is to see the performance of each protocol when encrypting significant amounts of data.

Furthermore, in a different set of tests, to ascertain that the Californium Library were communicating correctly, a Windows 10 computer with Wireshark sniffing tool was used to sniff packets sent between the server and client software and validate that the transferred networks packets were indeed encrypted with the expected protocols and contained the expected data. The total bytes transferred were also recorded with Wireshark on the same Windows setup. Using this method, we eliminate insecurities if a library reports wrong values. This makes it possible to verify that the recorded byte lengths are correct.

4   Results of the Practical Tests

A series of practical tests to determine performance and overhead between different protocols were performed.

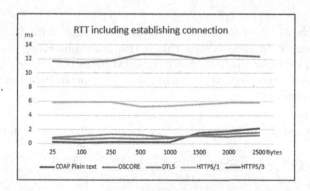

Fig. 3. Total time from establishing connection until complete data is received.

Table 2. Total bytes transferred from establishing connection until data is received.

Data bytes	CoAP plain	OSCORE	DTLS	HTTPS/1.1	HTTPS/3
25	133	158	1708	3703	10622
100	209	233	1783	4209	11123
500	609	633	2183	4610	11435
2500	3071	3196	4183	6530	13026

Figure 3 shows the total time in milliseconds for each protocol, for establishing a connection and receiving the given amount of bytes. Table 2 likewise show the total amount of transferred bytes, including overhead from establishing the connection, for given amounts of data for each protocol.

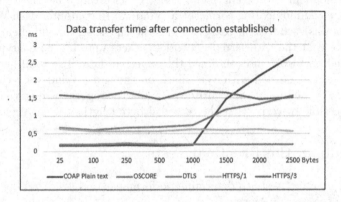

Fig. 4. Time from requesting data until received, after connection is established

Figure 4 shows the time required from the request until the data frame arrived. Important to note is that this is the time subtracted the connection establishment overhead. Table 3 shows the total bytes transferred, from request until data frame is received. Again, as in Fig. 3, subtracted the connection establishment overhead.

Table 3. Total bytes transferred from requesting data, after connection is established.

Data bytes	CoAP plain	OSCORE	DTLS	HTTPS/1.1	HTTPS/3
25	133	158	178	440	797
100	209	233	254	516	953
500	609	633	681	916	1753
2500	3071	3196	2655	2916	2973

5   Interpretation of Data

From Fig. 3 is seen a very large overhead of establishing connections over HTTPS. A surprising factor, however, is how much of a different there is between the HTTPS/3 and HTTPS/1.1 protocols. We would expect that HTTPS/3 should be faster than previous generations, partly by eliminating the TCP overhead, but at least for small amounts of data this is not the case.

In regard to OSCORE, Fig. 3 and Table 2, shows that OSCORE has a significantly lower overhead compared to the TLS based protocols. This is partly due to encrypting the content via a shared symmetrical key as no official methods of key negotiation has been decided yet. This means that there is no key negotiation at all in the test-setup of OSCORE and both sides already know the key to be used before the first communication between them. Figure 4 shows an interesting perspective however, as round-trip time when requesting data is actually significantly higher with OSCORE compared to DTLS and even HTTPS/1.1. This is in contrast to the speed increase that OSCORE has been observed to deliver, according to earlier, different performance measurements like in Fig. 5.

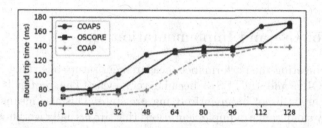

Fig. 5. Alternative measurement of OSCORE, CoAP/DTLS (COAPS) and CoAP Plain text (COAP) Round Trip Time. From: "Evaluating the performance of the OSCORE security protocol in constrained IoT environments" [12].

After a certain data size, the Californium implementations of DTLS and OSCORE fragment their packets automatically, disregarding the fact that the network can accommodate larger packets. In very constrained environments, the HTTPS header sizes might cause a problem. HTTPS headers can be very large and include a lot of, perhaps, unnecessary data [18]. Interesting to note is that the HTTPS/3 library, flupke, also fragments packets. While we see a large increase in data transfer time of OSCORE data transfers, the same issue does not occur with HTTPS/3. This is caused by the same thing that causes the HTTP/3 library to be significantly slower in establishing connections: HTTP/3 is capable of, and by default, opens multiple data channels between the client and server at once.

Having multiple data channels provides a significant boost when transferring large amounts of data between two end points, something that is often required in a desktop browser environment, and this is also why HTTPS/3 does not increase

```
QUIC        1232 Initial, DCID=956298a742fe1207, SCID=e6302e8a532ccafe, PKN: 0, CRYPTO, PADDING
QUIC         165 Retry, DCID=e6302e8a532ccafe, SCID=bac5aa10
QUIC        1233 Initial, DCID=bac5aa10, SCID=e6302e8a532ccafe, PKN: 1, CRYPTO, PADDING
QUIC        1284 Handshake, DCID=e6302e8a532ccafe, SCID=10dc552f
QUIC         259 Protected Payload (KP0), DCID=e6302e8a532ccafe
QUIC        1234 Initial, DCID=10dc552f, SCID=e6302e8a532ccafe, PKN: 2, ACK, PADDING
```

Fig. 6. Wireshark capture of flupke and Caddy establishing HTTPS/3 connection over QUIC in the test setup.

transfer time significantly when fragmenting data packets. Opening multiple data channels, however, also proves to be very disadvantageous when establishing a connection to a small device in a constrained network environment as large amounts of data are transferred in order to establish multiple data channels for no real benefits when transferring small chunks of data. Figure 6 shows multiple connections being established between the Caddy Server and the flupke HTTP/3 java library.

In the QUIC RFC [8], an arbitrary number of streams are allowed, this means that switching to a different implementation of QUIC might result in significantly lower overhead.

6   Ease of Use and Implementation

While implementing the performance measurement setup, one thing, specifically about OSCORE and HTTPS/3 became very clear. The protocols are newly defined and are still not in an entirely mature state. This also means that there is only a very small range of implementations that are actually working - and even between those that are working there seems to be significant caveats stopping the development of a functional application based upon these libraries.

For OSCORE, a few different libraries exist. Californium, CoAP.NET, aiocoap and libOSCORE have existed for a while and should be capable of a basic implementation of OSCORE [4]. Practically testing and working with these libraries, however, reveal that many of them are stagnant in a state where they cannot be implemented and have been for many months. Californium as a library cannot easily be compiled out of the box to a single functional library. Coap.NET no longer has a functional implementation of OSCORE. Aiocoap, while seemingly should have a basic implementation, cannot establish a connection between server and client and libOSCORE has never reached a maturity point where it can be implemented without significant development, even on its target platform of RIOT-OS.

The state of HTTPS/3 seems to be slightly better with more active development behind it. It does however suffer some of the same issues as OSCORE, being a new protocol and thus perhaps not mature enough. For Java, only a single implementation of a HTTPS/3 library seem to exist and only two serious attempts at QUIC implementations (kwik and Quiche4j), and of those two one of them, Quiche4j is also stagnant in a non-functional state.

Having no actively and fully developed libraries present, we got problems with these protocols - How can we be certain they are secure? How can we be certain they uphold the RFC itself? With these questions in mind, even if the specification of a protocol is secure, how can we be certain the implementation is secure as well?

7   Security of Protocols

Choosing between the different communication and encryption protocols results in a few different security concerns. In this section we will give a more in-depth overview of pros and cons for the different choices.

7.1   TLS

TLS is the backbone of HTTPS communication. As HTTPS is an extremely widespread communication protocol at this point, TLS is subject to a lot of different attempted (and sometimes successful) attacks. Some of the more recent large scale security breaches we have seen is for example the heartbleed vulnerability in OpenSSL [19]. It would allow an attacker to send a heartbeat with a message that was shorter than the stated length. A heartbeat is answered with the same message and same length. Because of this, the OpenSSL library would try to respond with the same message, but additionally also include any data stored in memory beyond the received message, in order to live up to the message length requirement. Leaked data can include sensitive information like credit cards, passwords and alike as that communication is all usually decoded in OpenSSL.

Many TLS attacks, like the aforementioned heartbleed attack, are directed towards the specific TLS library and not the TLS protocol itself. With TLS 1.3 in general, there are no known major security flaws, however this is not the case with older versions of TLS [20]. As long as an updated and widespread library is used and only the latest TLS is allowed, data transferred over TLS can be considered secure.

7.2   DTLS

DTLS is supposed to be almost entirely identical to TLS and the original RFC of DTLS is indeed only a description of the modifications to TLS. Because of this, in theory there should not be any security issues that are not present in TLS. It has, however, been proven that this is not the case.

DTLS is in many cases implemented entirely from scratch in security libraries, and being an extension to TLS, it can still claim to have the same security benefits and risk factors as TLS. The DTLS is often implemented separately from TLS, however, resulting in versions of DTLS that at times are lacking in patches to known security issues that are being discovered and fixed in TLS [21]. DTLS also follows the TLS versioning with DTLS 1.3 currently in proposal [22].

As DTLS 1.3 is still only proposed and not realized yet, though TLS 1.3 was released in 2018, current DTLS 1.2 implementations only comply to the security standards of the corresponding older versions of TLS, and not the widespread TLS 1.3 [23].

Another shortcoming of DTLS compared to TLS is referred to in the proposed DTLS 1.3 RFC itself: "The DTLS 1.3 protocol is intentionally based on the Transport Layer Security (TLS) 1.3 protocol and provides equivalent security guarantees with the exception of order protection/non-replayability [22]". This means DTLS does not by default enforce protection against replay and reordering attacks, it is entirely optional in a full implementation of DTLS whether countermeasures should be'taken against these types of attacks. Replay attacks can be a big security threat that can result in wrong, or perhaps even intentionally harmful information being delivered. An example could be an electric kettle that was told to turn off by the owner. A malicious third party could at an earlier point have sniffed the packet turning the kettle to 100° and 'replay' this message in order to turn on the kettle against the wishes of the owner.

7.3   OSCORE

OSCORE is a very different approach to securing data than the other mentioned protocols. Instead of encrypting the entire data stream, all of the headers of the CoAP or HTTP protocol are still transmitted entirely in plain text. This allows for a small amount of header data from the protocols to be leaked.

Fig. 7. The ASCII values of a local OSCORE packet. Underlined is the URI included in the "Uri-Host" CoAP option.

For example in Fig. 7 the host URI of the data requested is shown. This can be a security issue, as data encrypted only with OSCORE will leak different CoAP options, some worse than others. The "Uri-Host" for example, is for the proxies to forward the message and might leak the requested domain. Furthermore OSCORE also does not encrypt the CoAP token that identifies a response message from a request. This allows a malicious third party to identify responses to specific messages.

OSCORE is also lacking perfect forward secrecy as seen in Table 1. This effectively means that if the encryption key for the message is leaked, the entire conversation history can be decoded.

The two TLS based protocols, HTTPS and DTLS, support Perfect Forward Secrecy, which allows the communicating parties to exchange new encryption keys on a regular basis. This means that intruders that gain access to a single key will only be able to deduce a small portion of the data. Meanwhile, OSCORE does not have such an implementation, so a potential key breach is a large problem [2]. In regard to proxy vulnerabilities, all aforementioned protocols except OSCORE will have potential security breaches for each proxy station. HTTPS, however, has an advantage in that the receiving end is often HTTPS-based and therefore this issue affects DTLS the most.

Unlike DTLS, OSCORE does provide protection against replay attacks and for OSCORE this protection is not opt-in. With the aforementioned CoAP tokens it can also bind responses to specific requests which provides protection against maliciously injected responses as those would be discarded for a wrong or missing token.

As OSCORE is a relatively newly proposed protocol which currently is in production at very few locations, not a lot of security research has been done in regard to investigate vulnerabilities of OSCORE. While DTLS suffers from a lack of active development, so does OSCORE to a much bigger extent. Currently a very limited amount of libraries are available and not a lot of active development is being done on OSCORE. This results in a platform where, even if the protocol itself is secure, it is likely that vulnerabilities in the libraries will be discovered, but not immediately patched, leaving a gap in security.

8   Discussion

From our results we see that HTTPS has a higher overhead and processing time than any of the other protocols. Especially in cases where small amounts of data is to be transferred, HTTPS seems to be a counter intuitive choice considering the alternative CoAP solutions available. That being said, while the overhead of HTTPS might burden the device more than CoAP, there is a significant cost with introducing CoAP to the device as the amount of available libraries are severely limited compared to HTTPS. The DTLS based CoAP seemingly performs better than the OSCORE based solution in our tests, currently seems to be only a single entirely functional implementation of OSCORE, which is in Java, designed for desktop computers. No further tests have been made to verify this. While both the HTTPS and CoAP/DTLS based solutions will have to mitigate the same issue of proxies having to decrypt and reencrypt data, the proxies are often introduced in specifically in order to translate between CoAP devices and HTTPS-based devices. Considering this, while the same security issue exists in both of these platforms, it is likely a bigger issue in regard to CoAP than HTTPS.

Many IP-based devices have spare resources. In those cases it can be argued that the benefits of running a full HTTPS client on the device may outweigh much the potential gains of implementing something like CoAP. HTTPS will eliminate some of the reasons to use a proxy between the IoT device and the cloud service. Furthermore, the HTTPS protocol and libraries have a tendency to be more well-documented and widespread, which can ensure the security of the device and add stability. Devices in today's market are becoming increasingly more powerful and the networking solutions are becoming increasingly more performant with no significant battery hits, and if this trend continues, reasons for selecting CoAP might be worth considering.

CoAP is designed for IoT applications in very constrained environments. An argument can also be made that perhaps even using IP is, to a certain extent, overkill. Many different wireless protocols like Z-Wave, SigFox and LoRaWAN does not support IP at all, but instead implement their own protocol stack. In many cases, connecting device to an IP-based network might not make sense, which is also something to consider before investing in CoAP technology.

In the cases where IP is desired on a device that does not have resources to spare for HTTPS, it can be worthwhile to consider CoAP with DTLS or OSCORE. In these cases the potential use case must be considered. In some cases, where for example proxies are required to transfer data, the OSCORE model might make more sense, but in other cases the added security benefits of a more well-tested and perhaps secure protocol like DTLS might make more sense.

For scenarios where security has high priority but network resources are not abundant, it can also be worthwhile to consider that OSCORE and DTLS are not mutually exclusive. It might be a viable solution to encrypt packets with both OSCORE and DTLS. This will add load to the CPU, but the overhead in terms of total bytes transferred and time on the air will not be increased dramatically. This would allow for the replay and proxy protection of OSCORE while also pertaining the benefits of the DTLS protocol encrypting the entire message and adding perfect forward secrecy.

The tests show a general trend towards HTTPS/3 over QUIC being even heavier than HTTPS over TCP, so for limited devices, the HTTPS/3 protocol does not seem to make sense, though this might also be slightly due to the implementation of HTTPS/3. The QUIC protocol is designed with multiplexing of data streams in mind - and not a general optimization of overhead, which is clear from the results.

9   Conclusion

In this paper we have tested multiple different networking protocols, some designed with limited devices in mind, some not so much. Keeping in mind the test setup was not as constrained, We found that CoAP based solutions are faster and more performant than HTTP based solutions. Furthermore we found no significant performance advantages of OSCORE compared to DTLS, especially if establishing the connection is not factored in. We would also argue that HTTP/3 while implemented on top of UDP does not provide any significant advantages compared to HTTP/1.1 over TCP, but rather increases overhead and limits performance dramatically.

While the test results do indeed show advantageous conditions with regard to network overhead for the CoAP based protocols, the performance and networking overhead associated with HTTPS does not show enough of a disadvantage to justify using less widespread and potentially more insecure libraries that are perhaps unfinished or stagnant at best. Furthermore, it shows no significant advantages of using a CoAP/OSCORE combo over a HTTPS solution in a product, unless a very constrained network or MCU is being used, and in many of those cases, using the IP stack instead of other protocols specifically designed for limited devices might be worth reconsidering altogether.

In cases where CoAP is the chosen solution, we argue that it is possible to protect data with a combination of both DTLS and OSCORE as they can be used in combination rather than as alternatives.

References

1. Shelby, Z., Hartke, K., Bormann, C.: The constrained application protocol (CoAP). RFC 7252. IETF (2014)
2. Gündoğan, C., Amsüss, C., Schmidt, T.C., Wählisch, M.: IoT content object security with OSCORE and NDN: a first experimental comparison. In: Proceedings of 19th IFIP Networking. IEEE Press (2020)
3. Amazon Web Services Inc: Device communication protocols. https://docs.aws. amazon.com/iot/latest/developerguide/protocols.html. Accessed 23 Jan 2022
4. Jensen, J.C., Stormholt, A.R.: Survey and evaluation of OSCORE security and implementation. Unpublished Paper, Technical University of Denmark (2021)
5. Selander, G., Mattsson, J., Palombini, F., Seitz, L.: Object security for constrained RESTful environments (OSCORE). RFC 8613, IETF (2019)
6. Fielding, R., et al.: Hypertext transfer protocol - HTTP/1.1. RFC 2616, IETF (1999)
7. Rescorla, E.: HTTP Over TLS. RFC 2818, IETF (2000)
8. Iyengar, J., Thomson, M.: QUIC: a UDP-based multiplexed and secure transport. RFC 9000, IETF (2021)
9. Gündoğan, C., Kietzmann, P., Lenders, M., Petersen, H., Schmidt, T.C., Wählisch, M.: NDN, CoAP, and MQTT: a comparative measurement study in the IoT. In: Proceedings of ACM ICN. ACM (2018)
10. MQTT Version 5.0. Edited by Andrew Banks, Ed Briggs, Ken Borgendale, and Rahul Gupta. OASIS standard, 07 March 2019
11. Rescorla, E., Modadugu, N.: Datagram transport layer security version 1.2. RFC 6347, IETF (2012)
12. Gunnarsson, M., Brorsson, J., Palombini, F., Seitz, L., Tiloca, M.: Evaluating the performance of the OSCORE security protocol in constrained IoT environments. ScienceDirect (2020). https://www.sciencedirect.com/science/article/pii/S2542660520301645. Accessed 23 Jan 2022
13. Hristozov, S., Huber, M., Xu, L., Fietz, J., Liess, M., Sigl, G.: The cost of OSCORE and EDHOC for constrained devices. arXiv:2103.13832 (2021)
14. Eclipse Foundation: Eclipse Californium CoAP framework. https://www.eclipse. org/californium/. Accessed 23 Jan 2022
15. Caddy Server Project. https://caddyserver.com/. Accessed 23 Jan 2022
16. QUIC-Go project. https://github.com/lucas-clemente/quic-go. Accessed 23 Jan 2022
17. Flupke Project. https://bitbucket.org/pjtr/flupke. Accessed 23 Jan 2022
18. Gadient, P., Nierstrasz, O., Ghafari, M.: Security header fields in HTTP clients. arXiv:2111.03601 (2021)

19. CVE Mitre database. https://www.cve.org/CVERecord?id=CVE-2014-0160. Accessed 12 Apr 2022
20. Stebila, D.: Attacks on TLS. https://www.douglas.stebila.ca/files/research/presentations/tls-attacks/tls_attacks_table.pdf. Accessed 23 Jan 2022
21. AlFardan, N.J., Paterson, K.G.: Plaintext-recovery attacks against datagram TLS. https://www.isg.rhul.ac.uk/kp/dtls.pdf. Accessed 23 Jan 2022
22. Rescorla, E., Tschofenig, H., Modadugu, N.: The datagram transport layer security (DTLS) protocol version 1.3. draft-ietf-tls-dtls13-43, IETF (2021)
23. Qualys SSL Labs: SSL Pulse. https://www.ssllabs.com/ssl-pulse/. Accessed 23 Jan 2022
24. Ahmed, M., Akhtar, M.M.: Smart home: application using HTTP and MQTT as communication protocols. arXiv:2112.10339 (2021)

Author Index

Abduljabbar, Zaid Ameen   103
Al Sharji, Safiya   91
Al Shuaily, Huda   91
Aldarwish, Abdulla J. Y.   103
Al-Qasmi, Ahmed   91
Amaral, António   29, 66
Andersen, Birger   117

Biondo, Elias   76
Brito, Thadeu   76

Cardoso, António   39, 55

D'Orey, Frederico   39

Ehimwenma, Kennedy E.   91

Fernandes, Carlota   39
Figueiredo, Jorge   55

Impagliazzo, John   3

Kiesler, Natalie   3

Lima, José   76
Longras, Ana   66

Ma, Junchao   103
Maolood, Ismail Yaqub   103
Mendes, Isabel   29

Nakano, Alberto   76
Nedergaard, Kristofer   117
Nyangaresi, Vincent Omollo   103

Oliveira, Isabel   55

Pereira, Manuel Sousa   39
Pereira, Teresa   29, 66
Pocinho, Margarida   55

Rodrigues, Sandra   39

Sibahee, Mustafa A. Al   103
Singh, Bhupjit   117
Stavrou, Eliana   18

Printed in the United States
by Baker & Taylor Publisher Services